Icelandic Color Knitting

Rose - pattern insert knitting in a new light

Hélène Magnússon

Salka

Reykjavík 2007

Icelandic Color Knitting
Original title: *Rósaleppaprjón í nýju ljósi*
© Text: Hélène Magnússon 2006
© Knitting patterns and charts: Hélène Magnússon
© Photographs: Hélène and Skúli Magnússon, Signý Kolbeinsdóttir p. 9
and Arnaldur Halldórsson p. 64
Design: Hélène Magnússon
Layout: Ragnheiður Ingunn Ágústsdóttir
English translation: Orðabankinn sf.
Printed in Delo Tiskarna, Slovenia.

SALKA – Reykjavík – 2007

Table of Contents

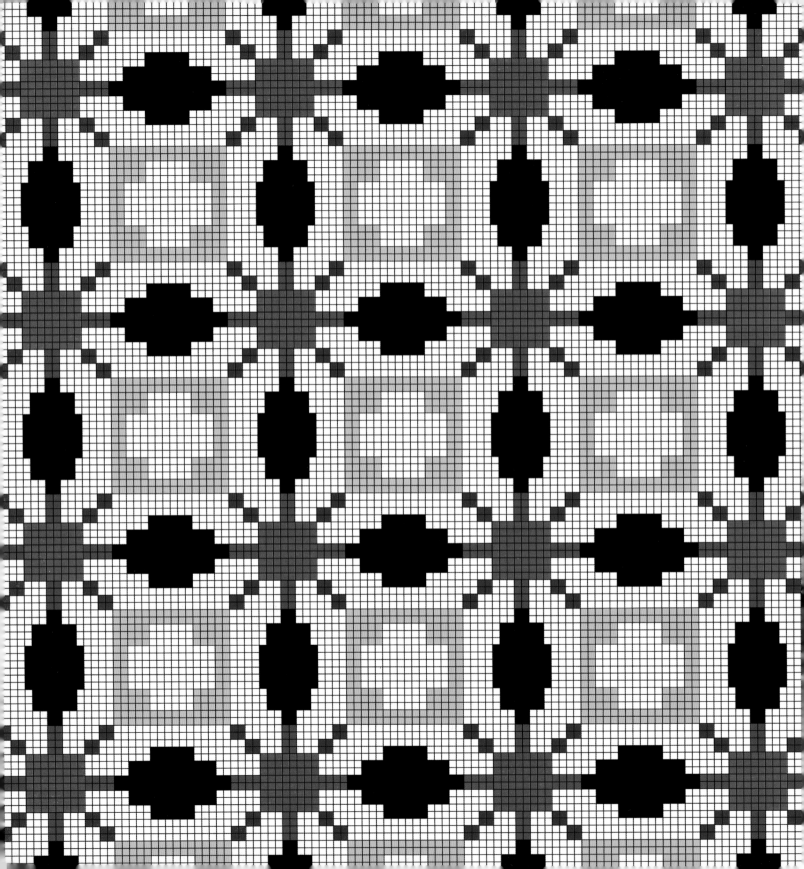

Preface

In recent years, Iceland has seen a great revival of interest in everything associated with national tradition, a trend that has not been limited to this country. Every nation's distinguishing characteristics have become less marked in recent decades, and many factors play a part in this: communication is much easier; there are no national borders in the Internet; most restrictions on travel have been lifted; there has been a tremendous increase in the range of goods for sale; we buy the ingredients for recipes from around the world in shops that are open more or less around the clock; and no matter where we go, people wear the same clothes that are sold in the same chain shops. The "year 2000 syndrome" also had a major impact. Everyone was supposed to become cosmopolitan, "cast in the same mold," before the new millennium began. The course we had taken was developing quickly, minimalism was at its height, and fashion was sleek and plain, displaying no particularly national traits.

But fortunately, human beings are more complicated than that. They have a strong need and desire to be seen as individuals, and throughout human history, personal adornment has been very important. In a society as small as the one we live in here in the north, the closure of the National Museum for 10 years was probably significant in this respect. The national consciousness, national traditions and folk art were put into cold storage, so to speak, and nothing really emerged to replace them. It was impossible to bring the Museum into the 20th century overnight - it took ten years to modernize it, give it the attractive form it now possesses, and make it accessible to the public, especially the youngest generation of artists and designers, who have developed a lively interest in the national heritage. Now, at the beginning of the 21st century, tradition is "cool." There is innovative music-making based on traditional sung poetry (*rímur*), a growing interest in the old Nordic religion, and Viking festivals are held throughout the country. There has been an interest in establishing contact with the descendants of Icelanders who emigrated to North America, and this interest has been reciprocated with the descendants of Icelandic immigrants visiting Iceland in search of their roots. There has also been a general upswing in tourism, and foreign visitors' interest in everything Icelandic has created a market for products with a traditional flair. The effort to reawaken a sense of national tradition seems to have been successful, because Icelanders have demonstrated great interest in museum exhibitions that are devoted to Icelandic history and design.

The fact that the lifetime of consumer goods is considerably shorter than used to be has put its mark on design. People used to keep things much longer: they simply lasted longer, people took better care of them and also had more respect for them. But today, if something stops working, we are quick to throw it aside and buy something new. Consumerism and the faster pace of life in general have taught us to do this from the time we were children. Our contemporary lifestyle demands never-ending production, a continuous cycle that is the essence of globalization. Parallel to innovation, there has been a tremendous increase in people's interest in the past, along with easier access to raw materials, which has in turn influenced designers' approaches to new products. Design is often based on need: an artist produces a simpler object that can be used more efficiently that those previously available. The designer derives his materials from a variety of sources. Nature, history, poetry, the sea - even the weather - might play a part in a task he sets for himself. An innovative product might also emerge from the joy of creating something new based on traditional craftsmanship.

Over the years, people have tended to belittle crafts, seeing design as a much superior area. But the two are actually inseparable - two sides of the same coin, if you will. There is now a rapid and growing appreciation of crafts, and it is very gratifying to see this book appear, as it takes an appreciative look at a traditional Icelandic craft. The knitting of woolen shoe inserts with rose patterns (*rósaleppaprjón*) is an artistic form of knitting that was developed by ordinary people in this country, and which preserved old motifs and color schemes that are unfamiliar to most of us today. The motifs used in the inserts support the theory that geometric forms and utility are the distinctive features of Nordic design. This book was written in the conviction that tried and tested design has a place in modern life, which it enriches through its beauty and history. I hope the book will become an essential addition to the collections of anyone interested in fashion, along with historians, collectors, and anyone else who might be inspired by it. For those who want to preserve the heritage of popular culture as seen in handicrafts and traditional design, the best option might not be to study this heritage in isolation but to allow it to develop further, each generation taking its own approach to past forms of expression. Globalization is now motivating people to look for each nation's distinguishing traits. Have we now discovered our unique traits in Icelandic design, or has the search for the true "Icelandic note" just begun?

María Ólafsdóttir, designer
maria@untitled.is

Introduction

In the spring of 1996, just a few months after I moved to Iceland, I took a job as a "hired girl" during the lambing season at the farm Hraun in Aðaldalur in the county of Suður-Þingeyjarsýsla. At Hraun, Jóhanna Steingrímsdóttir, the landlady's sister, gave me a pair of tiny sheepskin shoes with knitted inserts. This was the first time I had ever seen this type of footwear. A few years later, I began studying in the textile department of the Iceland Academy of the Arts and had the opportunity to do a project on Icelandic knitting. I recalled the inserts I had been given and decided to take a look at their history. I visited the National Museum as part of my research and was fascinated by the patterns, colors, and color schemes of the inserts I saw there. I then started taking photographs of the inserts kept in museums throughout the country, with the intention of collecting as many knitting motifs as I could and preserving them. In no time at all, I had photographs of more than 250 inserts, without having any very clear idea of how I intended to make use of them.

In 2004, I wrote a BA thesis on inserts under the guidance of Ágústa Kristófersdóttir of the Iceland Academy of the Arts, and inserts were also a source of inspiration when I designed a fashion line as my final project. The following summer, I was fortunate enough to win a scholarship from the Icelandic Student Innovation Fund to design hand-knitted garments using rose-pattern insert knitting under the supervision of fashion designer María Ólafsdóttir, and in cooperation with the Handknitting Association of Iceland. During my involvement in this work, I became steadily more convinced that the knowledge represented by the old inserts was about to be lost. I therefore continued working with this material in various ways, and this book gradually emerged. The purpose behind it was twofold: to call people's attention to and stimulate their interest in the wool insert tradition, and to encourage as many people as possible to make use of this treasure trove in a creative way. Above all, I wanted to do what I could to prevent this traditional knowledge from being lost.

In line with the book's twofold purpose, it is divided into two main sections, which are, however, closely connected. The first section contains detailed descriptions of inserts and a discussion of the history of the very old craft of rose-pattern insert knitting. This section consists largely of basic research. In the second part, there is an attempt to work with the old knitting tradition in an innovative way. This section contains knitting patterns which I have designed and made up on the basis of the designs and color schemes seen in the old inserts, along with an explanation of rose-pattern insert knitting and a description of the way the inserts were traditionally edged or bordered.

When designing garments, I have tried to remain true to the original color schemes of the inserts I chose, and the traditional methods used in making them. The inserts reappear in these new garments in various ways. Sometimes, I repeat the same motif several times, making a continuous pattern out of one insert-motif. At other times, I let the motif determine the shape the garment takes. And in still other patterns, I let inspiration decide how certain motifs will be arranged.

I would like to express my sincere thanks to everyone who has helped me in writing and publishing the book. Museum curators and personnel throughout the country were exceptionally helpful, providing me with very clear and useful information. I would like to thank my husband, Skúli Magnússon for all of his assistance. Curator Elsa E. Guðjónsson read over the first part of the book, and I owe her a particular debt of thanks for her many useful comments. My mother-in-law, Sylvía Guðmundsdóttir, read through the manuscript and suggested several improvements in the Icelandic. I would like to thank Sigríður Halldórsdóttir for teaching me to edge pieces of knitting in the traditional way called *slyngja* (band-weave edging), and Bryndís Eiríksdóttir, president of the Handknitting Association of Iceland for reading over the knitting patterns. The Handknitting Association of Iceland provided all of the yarn needed for making the model garments. Baldrún Kolfinna Jónsdóttir, Kristbjörg Steingrímsdóttir and Olga Hallgrímsdóttir helped me knit the prototypes, and family members and friends served as models for the photographs. And finally, I would like to thank the publisher Salka (Bókaútgáfan Salka) for believing in me and publishing a book on Icelandic knitting. As fate would have it, Hildur Hermóðsdóttir, director/CEO of Salka, turned out to be the daughter of Jóhanna Steingrímsdóttir, the woman who first introduced me to the fascinating world of inserts. So you could say that Hildur put the final touches to a process that her mother had set in motion 10 years before!

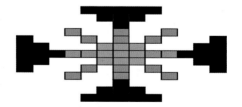

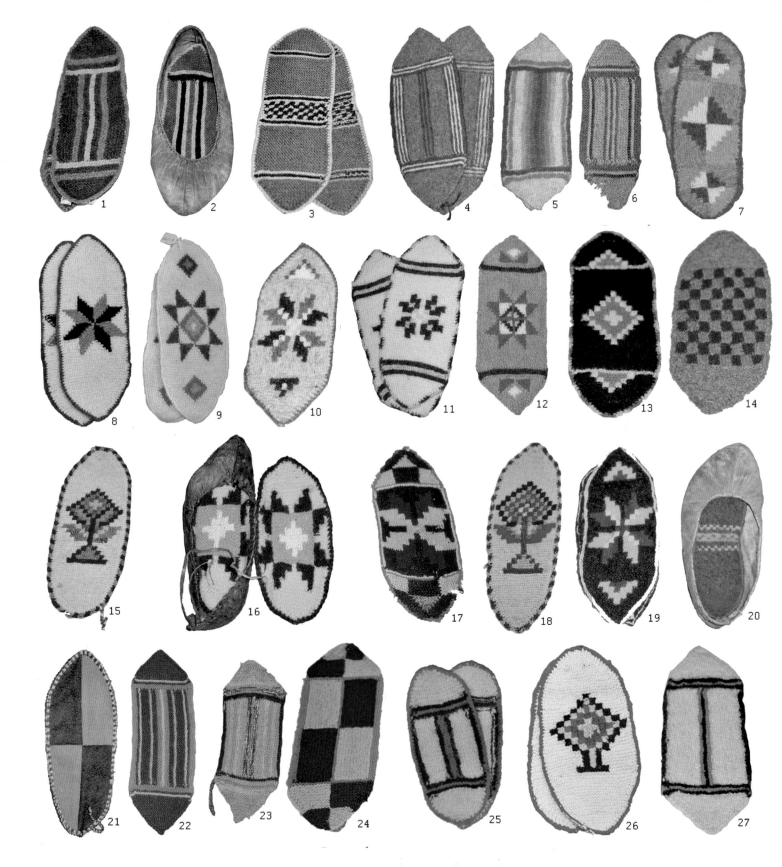

Inserts and rose - pattern insert knitting

Inserts p. 10: Textile Museum, Halldóra's room, Blönduós (1, 2, 3, 10, 13, 14, 17, 19, 24 and 27); Helga Þórarinsdóttir (4, 5, 6, 9, 11, 12, 22 and 23); Sigríður Halldórsdóttir (7); Icelandic Handcrafts Society (8); Skógar District Museum (15 and 18); Suður-Þingeyinga District Museum, Húsavík (16) and Grenjaðarstaðir (21); Akureyri Museum (20) and National Museum of Iceland, Ethnological Collections (25 and 26).

Knitting tradition

There has been a strong knitting tradition in Iceland ever since the end of the 16th century.[1] Knitting is believed to have originated in Egypt. From there it spread to all of North Africa and then to Spain. Catholic monks learned to knit and were instrumental in teaching this skill to Christian Europe.[2] Knowledge of knitting is thought to have come to Iceland with German, English, or Dutch merchants. The oldest written source indicating that knitting skills were known here is Bishop Guðbrandur's Bible translation, printed in Hólar in 1584, where Christ's robe is described as "knitted," not woven.[3] The oldest Icelandic knitted garments are mittens and a cap, which may have been made in the first half of the 16th century.[4] By the first half of the 17th century, knitted material had become a significant part of Icelandic exports.[5] Everyone knitted - children, men, and women. It is therefore surprising that there are so few sources that refer to Icelandic knitting. It is also surprising that the most prominent representative of Icelandic knitting today should be the famous Icelandic sweater (lopapeysa), which is only a little more than half a century old.

All of this led me to consider the woolen inserts. These are knitted insoles that were put into footwear such as soft shoes made of sheepskin or fishskin to make them warmer and more comfortable. They were colorful and presented a contrast to people's everyday clothing, which was normally dark in color or showed the natural colors of undyed wool. Inserts have a history that can shed light on Icelandic knitting traditions.

I will discuss the technique of making inserts, their different types, whether they can be considered a particularly Icelandic phenomenon, and if so, to what extent. I will also discuss the motifs used to decorate inserts. This survey[6] is based on an examination of inserts seen in the national and main district museums in Iceland during the period 1999-2005, when I collected photographs of more than 250 different inserts.[7] One

---

[1] Regarding knitting in Iceland in general see, for example, Þorkell Jóhannesson, *Ullariðnaður*, Iðnsaga Íslands II, Reykjavík 1943; Elsa E. Guðjónsson, *Prjón á Íslandi*, Reykjavík 1990; Fríður Ólafsdóttir, *Íslensk karlmannaföt 1740-1850*, Reykjavík 1999, pp. 22 to 26.

[2] Harte N.B. and Ponting K.G., *Cloth and Clothing in Medieval Europe, Essays in memory of Professor E.M. Carus-Wilson*, London 1983, p. 368.

[3] Inga Lárusdóttir, *Vefnaður, prjón og saumur*, Iðnsaga Íslands II, Reykjavík 1943, p. 12.

[4] Elsa E. Guðjónsson,"Fágæti úr fylgsnum jarðar, Fornleifar í þágu textíl- og búningarannsókna", *Skírnir: Ný tíðindi hins íslenzka bókmenntafélags*, 1992, no. 166. (spring issue), pp.7-40.

[5] According to business records, 72,230 pairs of socks were exported in the year 1624, along with 12,232 pairs of mittens. For details, see Jón J. Aðils, *Einokunarverzlun Dana á Íslandi 1602-1787*, Reykjavík 1971, pp. 500-501.

[6] This discussion is based on the author's BA thesis for the Iceland Academy of the Arts, advisor Ágústa Kristófersdóttir, March 2004.

[7] In some cases, identical inserts were found in the National Museum of Iceland and the Skógar District Museum. The reason for this was that the curator in Skógar, Þórður Tómasson, in some instances sent the National Musem one insert of each pair that he acquired. I have never found any other pairs of inserts that were identical.

important source of historical information was the replies to a questionnaire on shoemaking that the National Museum of Iceland, Ethnological Collections, sent to elderly people in the year 1964.[8]

1. Inserts

Description

Inserts were used as insoles in soft shoes and were seldom seen. It is therefore remarkable how beautiful many of them were, and how much care was taken in making them. It is also surprising how colorful inserts were at a time when clothing was made of undyed wool, or in somber brown, black, dark blue or gray colors. An amazing amount of work was put into making them, considering what a short lifetime most of them could be expected to have, as they quickly wore out when people walked on them. Inserts were practical things, and people used them in some form every day. They were utilitarian items, intended mainly for protecting the feet and keeping them warm.

Inserts and the techniques for making them were originally associated with soft shoes, and

Inserts in fishskin shoes: Textile Museum, Halldóra's room, Blönduós.

the use of inserts on a daily basis ceased shortly after people stopped using traditional footwear at the beginning of the 20th century.[9] Olga Hallgrímsdóttir, for example (born in Akureyri in 1917), remembers wearing sheepskin shoes with beautiful rose-pattern inserts as indoor shoes or house slippers as a child.[10]

---

[8] Unpublished source material in the National Museum of Iceland, Ethnological Collections. Replies to Survey 12: *Skógerð, Íslenskir skór, Skæðaskinn*, 1964.

[9] Often noted in ÞÞ (Þjóðháttaskráning Þjóðminjasafnsins), the National Museum's Ethnological Collections.

[10] Olga Hallgrímsdóttir in a conversation in September 2003.

Helga Þórarinsdóttir (born in 1927) used striped inserts in rubber boots when she was a little girl.[11] It can be assumed that inserts appeared at about the same time as soft shoes, as it is nearly impossible to wear this type of footwear without some kind of insole.

Little is known about the origin of soft shoes, and it is therefore difficult to say much about how the use of inserts came about. Most of the inserts found in museums stem from the first years of the 20th century. Knitted inserts are mentioned in a few sources, mainly the accounts of travelers to Iceland. The oldest example in a written source[12] dates from the early or mid-17th century and is found in a poem by the Reverend Guðmundur Erlendsson: "*Jleppa med alese skallt vtan slyngia.*"[13] Inserts were undoubtedly considered of little significance. Worn under the feet, they were almost never seen and not worth wasting many words on. In descriptions of Icelandic clothing, there is seldom reference to footwear, much less inserts in shoes. There are probably still many Icelanders who think they are of little consequence.

It might be possible to date the first use of inserts in Iceland by investigating when the knitting techniques used in making them first arrived in Iceland, and I will discuss that later. It is also appropriate to point out that inserts went by different names in different parts of the country and were sometimes given names that indicated the way they were made or the use they were put to. The most common term for them was *íleppar*, meaning inserted rags, with the variations *illeppar*, *ileppar*, and *skóleppar* (shoe inserts), but other words meaning rags or scraps of cloth were also used, *barðar* (South Iceland), *spjarir* (North Iceland), and *sparileppar*, *hversdagsleppar*, which refer to finer or "Sunday-best" and "everyday" inserts.[14] Several traditional expressions refer to inserts: *að vera undir íleppnum*, "to be under the insert," is used for a man who is dominated by his wife, or *að vera einhverjum íleppur í annan skó*,[15] "to be like an insert in one shoe for someone," which means that the person in question is an annoyance or causes difficulties for someone else. The National Museum´s Ethnological Collections list several metaphorical uses of the word *íleppur*, such as:

Hann var mér illeppur í annan skó, andskotinn sá arna.[16]
For me, he was like an insert in one shoe, the devil.

---

[11] Helga Þórarinsdóttir, handiwork instructor and teacher of traditional dancing, in a conversation in April 2005. She has held courses on making sheepskin shoes for the Icelandic Handcrafts Society.

[12] University of Iceland, *Orðabók Háskólans – ritmálsskrá*, lexis.hi.is, 31/01/2004.13 University of Iceland, Orðabók Háskólans – ritmálsskrá, lexis.hi.is, 31/01/2004.

[13] Guðmundur Erlendsson, *Grobbionsrímur séra Guðmundar Erlendssonar*, XIII 1-3 Reykjavík 1915-16-33, 47v, 17 fm.

[14] Often noted in ÞÞ.

[15] Both expressions are considered to date from the latter half of the 19th century. See Jón G. Friðjónsson, *Mergur málsins - Íslensk orðatiltæki, uppruni, saga og notkun*, Reykjavík 1993, p. 328.

[16] ÞÞ 1146.

Hann (eða hún) er ekkert annað en leppur í skónum hans (eða hennar).[17]

He (or she) is nothing but an insert in his (or her) shoe.

Ég skal verða þér leppur í annan skó.[18]

I shall be an insert in one of your shoes, or "I am going to make your life miserable."

Garter stitch inserts

Striped inserts are the simplest type of knitted inserts that have survived. They were used as everyday inserts and wore out quickly. They were called *barðar, skóbarðar*,[19] (rags, shoe rags), *barðaleppar*,[20] *prjónleppar*[21] (knitted rags), *garðaspjarir*[22] (garter inserts) or *randaloddar* (striped rag inserts)[23]. They were often kept in boxes called *plaggakassar*. A *plaggakassi* is a little box in which *plögg* (smaller items of clothing, gear), including finer footwear were kept.[24]

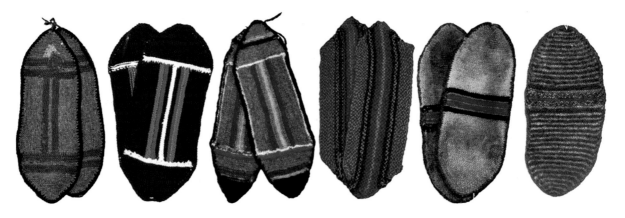

Striped inserts knitted in three stages: National Museum of Iceland, Ethnological Collections (1, 2, 3 and 5) and in one piece: Helga Þórarinsdóttir (4) and Árbær Museum (6).

[17] ÞÞ 1212.
[18] ÞÞ 1039.
[19] ÞÞ 1212.
[20] ÞÞ 1212.
[21] ÞÞ 1212.
[22] ÞÞ 985.
[23] ÞÞ 915.
[24] ÞÞ 990.

These inserts were normally knitted in three stages using garter stitch. They were called *langrandaleppar*[25] or *langröndóttir leppar*[26] (long-striped inserts). The middle section was knitted first, the stitches picked up at the edge, and then the tips (front and back sections) knitted onto the middle section. They were symmetrical in form, and there was usually no difference between the front and back sections. The middle section had no special name, but it was sometimes called *leppsmiðja*.[27] The tips were called *tota*,[28] *hæltota*[29] and *tátota*,[30] (referring to heel and toe); *húfur*,[31] *húa*,[32] *lepphúfur*,[33] (caps); *rassar*,[34] *barðarassar*,[35] (rumps); *endar*[36] (ends) or *gaflar* (gables).[37]

Striped inserts were also knitted in one piece from heel to toe. These were called *þverröndóttir*[38] or *þvergörðóttir*[39] (meaning that they were knit in a single direction). There was a greater risk of these inserts stretching, becoming too long, or losing their shape in some other way. They had decorative stripes only in the middle section. Some inserts were also knitted widthwise in one piece, knitting from one side to the other, with corresponding increases and decreases and narrowed at each end in order to form points. These inserts were decorated with oblong stripes in the middle.

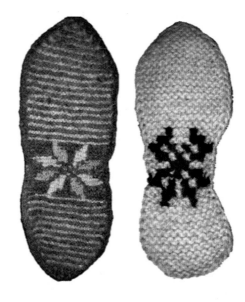

Rose-pattern inserts knitted to the shape of the foot: Suður-Þingeyinga District Museum, Grenjaðarstaðir (1) and Húsavík (2).

---

[25] ÞÞ 1040.

[26] Often noted in ÞÞ.

[27] ÞÞ 987 and 1210.

[28] Often noted in ÞÞ.

[29] ÞÞ 932, 7225, 7229 and 7230.

[30] ÞÞ 1006, 7225, 7229, 7230, 7232, 7233 and 7258.

[31] ÞÞ 915, 989, 1719 and 7254.

[32] ÞÞ 930.

[33] ÞÞ 971 and 1210.

[34] ÞÞ 951, 1124 and 7254.

[35] ÞÞ 947.

[36] ÞÞ 946, 947 and 976.

[37] ÞÞ 1124.

[38] Often noted in ÞÞ.

[39] ÞÞ 1210.

Sometimes, inserts were also knitted to the shape of the foot, making them narrower at the instep and wider at the toes.[40] Striped inserts were relatively simple to make. Children were often taught to knit by having them make striped inserts.[41] "Many children began by knitting what was called a "scarf for the cat," which was just a strip of knitted material. Then they moved on to inserts," said Haraldur Matthíasson from Árnessýsla county (born 1908).[42] Guðríður Þorleifsdóttir from Vestur-Ísafjarðarsýsla county (born 1886) remembers the inserts she knitted as a child. "When I was five or six years old, wooden knitting needles were made for me, which I was very fond of. I knitted inserts, white ones with red stripes, which were thought very beautiful, and my brother Jón made this verse about me:

Furðu smáu fingurnir
fínir eru að prjóna
litla mjög og laglega
leppa inn í skóna.[43]

Such tiny fingers
skilled at knitting
inserts for shoes,
so small and beautiful.

Decorative inserts knitted in garter stitch, such as *rósaíleppar*,[44] *rósabarðar*,[45] (rose-patterned inserts), were worn only on special occasions. They were kept in clothes chests with people's best pair of shoes.[46] Everyone liked to own a beautiful pair of inserts with a decorative pattern for Sunday best.[47] Such inserts were considered a good gift and were always very welcome. Girls gave the "boys they were friends with" rose-patterned inserts, said Snjólaug Hjörleifsdóttir from Norður-Múlasýsla county (born 1911).[48] They were often given as gifts on the first day of summer (celebrated in Iceland to this day), at Christmas, and

---

[40] ÞÞ 7230.
[41] Often noted in ÞÞ.
[42] ÞÞ 1124.
[43] ÞÞ 955.
[44] ÞÞ 981, 7229 and 7233.
[45] ÞÞ 924, 999, 1039 and 1540.
[46] Often noted in ÞÞ.
[47] Hulda Á. Stefánsdóttir, "Um íslenskan klæðnað", *Hugur og Hönd, Rit Heimilisiðnaðarfélags Íslands*, Reykjavík 1979.
[48] ÞÞ 7234.

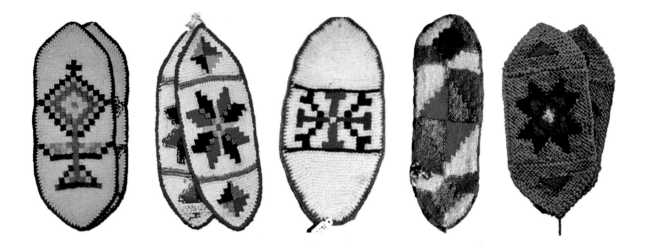

Colorful rose-pattern inserts: Sigríður Halldórsdóttir (1), National Museum of Iceland, Ethnological Collections (2 and 4), Skógar District Museum (3) and Rannveig Helgadóttir (5).

for birthdays, after it became customary to give such gifts in Iceland. The owner's initials were sometimes embroidered in the tips of the inserts.[49] "Handmade inserts, willingly given, were a memento of the person who made them, and were often as welcome as any expensive gift bought in a store," said Sigurður Egilsson from Suður-Þingeyjarsýsla county (born 1892).[50]

> Gömul nú ég orðin er,
> ástar finn þó stingi harða.
> Til sanninda ég sendi þér,
> sjónlaus þessa ljótu barða.[51]

> I may be old now, but I can still
> feel the sharp pangs of love.
> As proof, I send you,
> sightless, these ugly rags.

Rose-patterned inserts and other decorative inserts were either knitted using garter stitch in three stages or in one piece, from heel to toe, and sometimes to fit the shape of the foot. Many colorful

[49] For example, ÞÞ 1000.
[50] ÞÞ 1009.
[51] Rhyme quoted in ÞÞ 964.

patterns were used: roses in several forms, such as eight-petal roses, wind roses, step roses, hammer roses; a pattern in the shape of a flowerpot, an hourglass, a spiked mace or club called *högnakylfa*, and diamond-shapes, the latter inserts sometimes being called "diamond inserts" *tíglaleppar*.[52] The main motif usually appeared in the middle, the tips being decorated with stripes, part of the main pattern, some other embellishment, or left plain. Sometimes, only the tips of the inserts had a knitted pattern.[53] There are also examples of decorative borders, and of leaves or zig-zag patterns on either side of the rose in the middle.[54]

The inserts I have seen have up to eight different colors. The pattern is often made up of small squares, two stitches and two garters (four rows). Eight-petal roses were the most common pattern, and knitted patterns were sometimes combined with cross-stitch.[55]

Rose-pattern inserts with flower-pot motif and cross-stitch: Textile Museum, Halldóra's room, Blönduós.

The knitting technique called intarsia was used in making inserts. This was originally an Italian term, dating from 1863, for inlaid decoration in wood. The term has gradually come to be used in other contexts as well, and in connection with knitting since 1957.[56] In Iceland, it is called "motif knitting", (*myndprjón*). Rose-pattern insert knitting (*rósaleppaprjón*), is particular in that the motifs are done in garter stitch.[57]

In motif knitting, a new color of yarn is drawn over the yarn that

Example of intarsia technique: rose-pattern inserts, right side, wrong side, Akureyri Museum.

[52] ÞÞ 936, 949 and 1069.

[53] ÞÞ 7233.

[54] ÞÞ 952 and 973.

[55] Inserts belonging to the Textile Museum, Halldór's room, Blönduós.

[56] Rutt, Richard, see earlier ref., p. 228.

[57] Þórdís Kristleifsdóttir, "Rósaleppaprjón – séríslenskt myndprjón?", *Hugur og Hönd, Rit Heimilisiðnaðarfélags Íslands*, Reykavík 1996.

has been used so far. This has to be done in every row while changing color in order to prevent gaps. A special bobbin or small ball of yarn is needed for each block of color. You have to knit back and forth, because otherwise, the yarn that is to be used will end up on the wrong side of the block of color that is to be added. Rose-pattern insert knitting is probably the only example of knitting back and forth in Icelandic handiwork, as most knitting was circular.[58] The method is in fact simple, but it can become quite complicated when many colors are used, as there are then many bobbins, which are difficult to handle. Up to 15 bobbins could have been in use in one row in some of the inserts I have seen.

Children were often taught decorative knitting by having them knit simple hourglass motifs.[59] But not everyone could do rose-pattern insert knitting. These were mainly made by women who were very skilled in knitting, as rose-pattern inserts were considered artistic handiwork.[60]

Band-weave edged inserts

Inserts with a band-woven edge were also finer inserts, for special occasions. They were usually knitted two together in the round, using Fair-Isle knitting with stocking stitch and then cut in the middle. Four inserts, i.e. two pairs, may sometimes have been knitted at the same time on four needles.[61] [62] When doing Fair-Isle knitting, the yarn runs across the wrong side of the work, which is usually knitted in the round (this is actually always the case in the Nordic countries).[63] Inserts with band-woven edges were especially common in North Iceland. They were lined with wool or linen and edged with a narrow woven band.

The Icelandic terms *slyngja* or *slengja*[64] were used for a type of finger weaving. It is one of the most primitive and simplest kinds, also done with the help of one foot (*fótvefnaður*).[65]

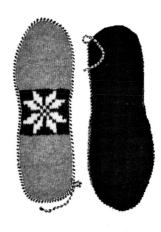

Band-weave edged inserts: Icelandic Handcrafts Society. Right side out, wrong side out.

[58] Elsa E. Guðjónsson in a conversation in January 2004. Elsa is a specialist in Icelandic textiles. The author refers to her articles and books in several places in this survey.
[59] ÞÞ 1540 and 7257.
[60] Often noted in ÞÞ.
[61] The question was asked in the National Museum's survey, but no one had ever heard of it.
[62] Helga Þórarinsdóttir, earlier ref., had heard of a woman who could do this, but she could not give the author any exact information.
[63] Gibson-Roberts, Priscilla A., *Knitting in the old way*, Colorado.
[64] ÞÞ 985 and 7215.
[65] Ryall, Pierre, *Le tissage à la main*, Presse de l'Est, Montbéliard, no date.

In Iceland, bands were woven for various uses, such as garters and apron bands.[66] Women who did not know the technique of tablet weaving or did not have the opportunity to do it, did finger weaving.[67] The special characteristic of Icelandic *slynging* is that it incorporates both sewing and weaving simultaneously. Two people sometimes worked together.[68] In 17th-century sources, there are examples of altar cloths [69] and a chasuble done with band-weave edging[70] but all other examples of *slynging* involve inserts.[71] Six to eight threads were woven together, in two colors, often alternating dark and light colors. It was considered

beautiful to use the same colors as in the pattern in the middle of the inserts.[72] There were not very many different motifs. These consisted mainly of roses, eight-petal roses, and stripes. I know one example of a hammer rose.[73] The use of more than two or three colors was rare. The inserts were usually adapted to the shape of the foot by felting, and the middle section with the pattern was felted more than the front and rear sections. A great deal of work was put into edging inserts with band-weaving, and even though the techniques used were simple, it was considered a very artistic form of handiwork, as it was very time-consuming.[74] Sólveig Indriðadóttir from Þingeyjarsýsla county (born 1910) said of her grandmother: "Beautiful band-weave

Band-weave edged inserts: Elsa E. Guðjónsson (1), Akureyri Museum (2) and Suður-Þingeyinga District Museum, Húsavík (3).

[66] Halldóra Bjarnadóttir, *Vefnaður á íslenskum heimilum,* Reykjavík 1966, p. 98 and p. 184.

[67] Jónas Jónasson, *Íslenzkir þjóðhættir,* Reykjavík 1961, p. 128.

[68] ÞÞ 1069.

[69] National Archives of Iceland, Bbps, Copenhagen 1878, AII 10, 53r (1642), AII 8, 478 (1672).

[70] National Archives of Iceland, Bbps, Copenhagen 1878, AII 7, 156 (1662).

[71] University of Iceland, *Orðabók Háskólans – ritmálsskrá,* lexis.hi.is, 31/01/2004.

[72] Sigríður Halldórsdóttir, "Slyngdir leppar", *Hugur og Hönd, Rit Heimilisiðnaðarfélags Íslands,* Reykjavík 1973.

[73] ÞÞ 1410.

[74] Guðmundur Þorsteinsson frá Lundi, *Horfnir starfshættir og leiftur frá liðnum öldum,* Reykjavík 1975, pp. 40-41.

edged inserts [were] her specialty, and in her spare time, after the autumn sheep-slaughtering and until Christmas, she was kept very busy making them."[75] Today, few people know how to do the *slynging*, and the technique has almost been forgotten.

Sewn inserts

Inserts were not always knitted. There were sewn inserts called *stykkjaleppar* or *stykkjaspjarir* (piece inserts), and they were often made of four pieces of cloth in two to four colors, often red or black, in a crosswise arrangement. Relatively small scraps of material could be used to make these inserts. They had a continuous band-woven edge. Sometimes, blanket-stitch was also used. Piece inserts were not intended for ordinary use and were considered appropriate gifts when spending holidays as a guest at a farm (*orlofsgjöf*).[76]

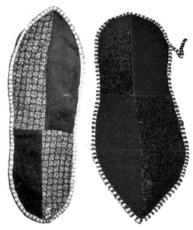

Piece inserts: Suður-Þingeyinga District Museum, Grenjaðarstaðir (1) and Textile Museum, Halldóra's room, Blönduós (2.).

There were also inserts of only one color, usually black. They had all kinds of embellishments, such as roses, diamond-shaped motifs, or stripes in flat embroidery, braided embroidery, contour-stitch or chain stitch.[77] These were made of yarn ends in all kinds of beautiful colors. These inserts had no special name, but they were sometimes called *vaðmálsleppar*,[78] (homespun wool inserts), *tauleppar*[79] (cloth inserts) or rose-pattern inserts when they were embroidered with roses. Þorbjörg R. Pálsdóttir of Suður-Múlasýsla county (born 1885) described inserts that "some women made out of [. . .] scraps of black cloth or fine black homespun wool and embroidered roses in the middle with yarn or loose-spun wool, decorating the ends with cross-stitch in various colors."[80] Hallfríður Rósantsdóttir from Eyjafjarðarsýsla county (born 1898) remembers the first inserts she made: "I think I was six or seven years old. They were yellow or

[75] ÞÞ 4200.

[76] Jónas Jónasson, see earlier ref.

[77] ÞÞ 985, 1018, 1059, 7215, 7232 and 7260.

[78] ÞÞ 1059.

[79] ÞÞ 930.

[80] ÞÞ 985.

brown, and I collected all kinds of yarn ends to sew into them. I liked the bits of red and green yarn the best. For me, they were the prettiest. I don't think I've ever been as proud of anything I've sewed. I gave the inserts to my mother."[81] I have never seen any inserts like the ones described here.

And finally, there were sewn inserts called *stangaðir leppar* (stitched inserts). They would scarcely have been called attractive, they were intended simply for comfort, not for decoration. They were sewn together out of scraps of wool, woolen cloth, discarded clothing, scraps of knitting, or other leftovers, and consisted of two or three layers, depending on the thickness of the material used. "If there was more than one layer of knitted material, you had to make sure that they were placed athwart each other, so they wouldn't stretch so much," said Sigurjón Erlendsson from Mýrarsýsla county (born 1897).[82] Burlap was sometimes used as well, and according to Guðlaugur Jónsson from Hnappadalssýsla county (born 1895) "a burlap insert was the most practical" and least likely to slip when water got into leather socks/ hose (*skinnsokka*).[83]

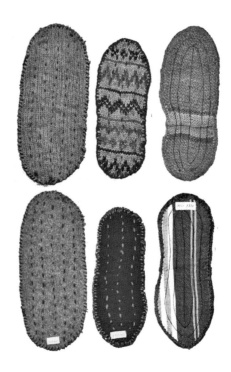

Stitched inserts, right side and wrong side out: National Museum of Iceland (1 and 2) and Akureyri Museum (3.).

Stitched inserts were often cut to the size of the foot. They had piping around the edges and lengthwise stitching. They were sometimes edged with blanket-stitch [84] or yarn ends placed over the edge of the insert and cast over.[85] These were not considered very good-quality inserts, as I said above, but they could be made relatively quickly. They were a kind of everyday insert, as it was impossible to wear

[81] ÞÞ 7215.
[82] ÞÞ 952.
[83] ÞÞ 1212.
[84] ÞÞ 1040.
[85] ÞÞ 915, 928, 1002, 7215, 7218, 7225, 7230 and 7232.

soft shoes without some kind of insert. An old woman called Spjara-Sólveig (Rag-Sólveig) put it very well:

Allt vill lagið hafa, þó það sé ekki nema spjör.[86]
Everything must be done properly, even a trifle like an insert.

These inserts were often used in the shoes people wore when working in the field or pasture (*engjaskór, smalaskór*).[87] They were given various names that referred to the way they were made - sewn rather than knitted - and the materials used, such as scraps and rags: *stagleppar,*[88] *staglaðir leppar,*[89] *stangleppar,*[90] *stangaðir leppar,*[91] *tuskuleppar,*[92] *tuskubarðar,*[93] *tauleppar,*[94] *stangdulur,*[95] *stangspjarir,*[96] *stöngur*[97] and *loddar.*[98] The last were derogatory terms for poor-quality inserts, according to Sigurjón Erlendsson from Mýrarsýsla county (born 1889).[99] At the beginning of the 20th century, when traditional soft shoes were disappearing from use, stitched inserts were sometimes made with sewing machines for use in rubber footwear.

Technical aspects of making inserts

There were no knitting patterns for inserts, no specific instructions concerning the number of stitches, decreases, increases, number of rows, etc.[100] This depended on the person for whom the inserts were intended and the type of yarn used, among other things.

The type of yarn used for knitting was important. Everyday inserts were often knitted tightly on large needles in order to make them as thick, strong, and warm as possible.[101] They were knitted from rough yarn

---

[86] Guðmundur Þorsteinsson, see earlier ref.

[87] ÞÞ 1069.

[88] ÞÞ 987, 952, 1007 and 1069.

[89] ÞÞ 1001.

[90] ÞÞ 1071.

[91] ÞÞ 917, 929, 955, 979, 993, 1000, 1059, 1069, 1017, 1212 and 7401.

[92] ÞÞ 976, 979, 1124, 7233 and 7256.

[93] ÞÞ 947, 964 and 1039.

[94] ÞÞ 930.

[95] ÞÞ 971, 993 and 1210.

[96] Guðmundur Þorsteinsson, see earlier ref., and ÞÞ 928, 932, 940, 945, 985, 991, 1002, 1082, 1410 and 3818.

[97] Jón Helgason and Stefán Einarsson, *Breiðdæla: Drög til sögu Breiðdals,* Reykjavík 1948, p. 170.

[98] ÞÞ 915, 928, 991, 1002, 1082, 1410, 3818, 7229, 7254 and 7258.

[99] ÞÞ 952.

[100] Mentioned in ÞÞ.

[101] Guðmundur Þorsteinsson, see earlier ref., and ÞÞ 7231.

(*togband*) or a yarn consisting of different types of wool, (*upp með öllu saman*)[102] spring and autumn wool being mixed together.[103] "Autumn wool was wool sheared from lambskin. It has little *tog* (the rougher outer coat of wool, longer and more resilient) and it tended to full more than the spring wool," said Lára and Karen Sigurðardóttir from Norður-Þingeyjarsýsla county (born 1905 and 1893).[104] Poor-quality yarn was also sometimes used, spun from left-over wool.[105] But inserts for special occasions were tightly knit on fine needles from fine yarn, for example, from good soft inner-coat yarn (*þelband*). Appearance was the most important thing when knitting such finer inserts, because they were not used very often.

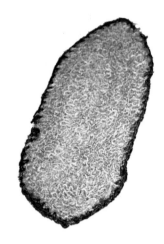

Insert made of horsehair: Textile Museum, Halldóra's room, Blönduós.

> *Maður spyr nú ekki að sparileppunum.*[106]
> Of course nothing compares to the Sunday-best inserts.

There are examples of horsehair inserts. These were "softer under the foot, warmer, and did not stay wet," said Guðlaugur Jónsson (born 1895).[107] They were often put into shoes that were worn with leather socks/hose (*skinnsokkar*). This was done, because feet tended to slip in soft skin shoes, especially if leather hose was also worn, and the shoes had got wet.[108] Horsehair inserts were also sometimes used under wool inserts, meaning that two inserts were used at the same time. If horsehair was used, it was spun on spindles like for rope, although it was finer, and the inserts were then knit in the usual way.[109]

[102] ÞÞ 947.

[103] Áslaug Sverrisdóttir, then curator of Árbær Museum, in a conversation in January 2004.

[104] ÞÞ 7232.

[105] ÞÞ 1039.

[106] Expression mentioned in ÞÞ 1146.

[107] ÞÞ 1212.

[108] ÞÞ 987.

[109] ÞÞ 1212.

As noted above, a variety of colors were used in the inserts. In the days when they were in common use, no colored yarn could be wasted. "Left-over yarn was highly suitable for knitting inserts, you could even make use of the short ends of a skein," said Sigurður Egilsson (born 1892).[110] Undyed wool in natural colors was used, also wool that had been dyed using Icelandic plants, as well as imported manufacture-dyed yarn from the 19th century.[111] When wool was dyed at home, the left-over dye was used to color the rough wool (*togband*) used for inserts. "This often produced a considerable variation in color, and the children liked working with this," said Ingibjörg Finnsdóttir from Strandasýsla county (born 1900).[112] Imported yarn was also used. There do not seem to have been any hard and fast rules about the colors used for inserts. This was decided by individual taste. A greater number of colors or combinations of colors increased the variation in the patterns used. I have to say at this point that it was the colors and color combinations of the inserts that originally caught my attention.

A variety of color and color combinations give a very different appearance to the same pattern. Rose-pattern inserts: Textile Museum, Halldóra's room, Blönduós (1 and 4), Skógar District Museum (2) and National Museum of Iceland, Ethnological Collections (3).

[110] ÞÞ 1009.
[111] Fríður Ólafsdóttir, see earlier ref., p. 24.
[112] ÞÞ 1069.

As mentioned above, most inserts were knitted in garter stitch. Bjargey Pétursdóttir from Norður-Ísafjarðarsýsla county (born 1902) had heard the name *hryggjaprjón* in which one *hryggur* (spine) consisted of two rows back and forth.[113] Garter stitch ensures that a great deal of air is captured in the inserts, which makes them warmer. Garter stitch also prevented inserts from rolling up, and then they did not need to be lined in order to keep them flat. However, I do know of two examples of garter-stitch inserts with linings.[114][115] Torfhildur Sigmundsdóttir of Norður-Múlasýsla county (born 1906) had seen examples of inserts where stocking stitch was used in the middle of the insert, and garter stitch in the tips.[116]

Inserts with band-weave edges, *slyngdir leppar*, were knitted using stocking stitch and then lined to keep them flat and prevent their rolling up. Torfhildur Sigmundsdóttir said some people knitted double-layer inserts and then it was not necessary to line them. She did not say whether these inserts were edged with band-weave. I have only found one example of this type of insert, and there was no woven edge.[117]

Elsa E. Guðjónsson, former curator of the Textiles and costume department of the National Museum of Iceland, told me about crocheted inserts owned by the Danish National Museum in Copenhagen.[118] I have not heard of any other examples of crocheted inserts.

People crocheted around the inserts so that they would keep their shape better and not stretch as much. Inserts were often knitted with a slip stitch (the first stitch of each row left unknit).[119] "People thought this made the edge prettier and it was also easier to crochet around the insert," according to Haraldur Matthíasson (born 1908).[120]

[113] ÞÞ 973.

[114] Jón Helgason and Stefán Einarsson, see earlier ref., p. 170: "Inserts done in garter stitch and lined were for everyday use."

[115] Inserts no. 1965-86: National Museum of Iceland, Ethnological Collections.

[116] ÞÞ 7233.

[117] Inserts no. 1962-214: National Museum of Iceland, Ethnological Collections.

[118] Hald, Margrethe, *Primitive shoes, An Archeological-Ethnological Study Based upon Shoe Finds from the Jutland peninsula*, National Museum of Denmark, Copenhagen 1972, p. 169

[119] ÞÞ 999 and 1124.

[120] ÞÞ 1124.

If inserts were too narrow, a few rows might be crocheted around them to make them wider. Sometimes these rows were knitted rather than crocheted. Then "stitches were picked up all around the insert, using four needles, and one or two garters knit," explained Sigurjón Erlendsson (born 1889).[121] If crocheting was done in two colors, this was called *stykkjótt*.[122]

Rose-pattern inserts with a knitted edge: Elsa E. Guðjóns-son (1) and rose-pattern inserts with a crocheted border in two colors (*stykkjóttir*): National Museum of Iceland, Ethnological Collections (2).

Most inserts had a cord (*tengsli*) with which to tie them together and hang them up to dry, for example on a nail in a beam in the kitchen.[123] It was also good to tie them together when washing them, so they were less likely to get lost. These cords were also called *tengslar*,[124] *hankar*,[125] *vindingar*,[126] *lindar*,[127] *stög*,[128] *snúrur*,[129] *lengjur*[130] or *endar*[131] (denoting different connections, loops, twists, bands, lines, lengths or ends).

The cords were made of strands that were braided or twisted together and the ensuing cord was attached to the insert at the point where the middle section and tip met. Sigríður Bogadóttir from Austur-Barðastrandarsýsla county (born 1907) tells us how this was done: "Four to six 20 cm long ends of the yarn

[121] ÞÞ 952.
[122] For example: ÞÞ 955 and 1018.
[123] ÞÞ 952.
[124] ÞÞ 7215.
[125] ÞÞ 952 and 7215.
[126] ÞÞ 917, 930, 973 and 976.
[127] ÞÞ 1212.
[128] ÞÞ 1018.
[129] ÞÞ 990.
[130] ÞÞ 7232 and 7233.
[131] ÞÞ 7229.

used for the insert were cut off and twisted together, a knot was tied at both ends, and they were cut in half in the middle, and threaded into each insert using a lacing needle at the beginning of the tip."[132] "It was also possible to attach the cord at the middle of the heel, but then they tended to work their way up out of the shoe, and people thought that was ugly," adds Eiríkur Einarsson from Árnessýsla county (born 1898).[133] The cords were often made at the same time as the border was crocheted around the insert or the band-weave edge attached.[134] "The cords were then laid under the insert when it was in the shoe," says Hallfríður Rósantsdóttir, mentioned above (born 1898).[135]

Most of the inserts were felted, but not in the conventional way. Ingibjörg Finnsdóttir (born 1900) explained this as follows: "They were very loosely threaded together at the edges, and washed and felted while they were basted together like this, so that they acquired the same shape."[136] When felting was finished, they were laid one over the other, and someone sat or lay on them over night. This was done with most knitted material.[137] After this treatment, they were smooth and had a nice finish.

Inserts for special occasions were felted with particular care. Guðlaugur Jónsson (born 1895) describes this as follows: the inserts were "washed and treated in a way that was called napping.

Felted everyday insert: Skógar District Museum.

[132] ÞÞ 976.
[133] ÞÞ 999.
[134] Often noted in ÞÞ.
[135] ÞÞ 7215.
[136] ÞÞ 1069.
[137] Jónas Jónasson, see earlier ref.

They were kneaded or rubbed to raise the nap. Then they were laid under the bedclothes in order to press and dry them."[138]

The way inserts were put into shoes mattered. Haraldur Matthíasson (born 1908) said: "It was thought that the right way to do this was to take the front end of the insert between the thumb, index finger, and middle finger, put the insert into the shoe, and then push it forward into the toe of the shoe with the index finger, middle finger, and ring finger. Some people folded the insert in two and stuck it into the shoe. That was considered rather crude."[139]

2. Inserts, a uniquely Icelandic phenomenon?

Uniquely Icelandic inserts?

Footwear has a long history. The first shoes are thought to have been foot-wrappings. People eventually started cutting material, cloth or skin and sewing it together to make shoes. This type of footwear was common all over the world.[140] Soft shoes were used not only in Iceland, but also by the native peoples of North America, and by peasants in Russia and the Baltic countries, to name just a few examples.[141] These shoes all needed some kind of insert, especially in cold climates. Inserts also served the purpose of protecting the feet when wearing these thin shoes, and they also helped make them more comfortable when it was hot and people's feet sweated.

Straw was commonly used for inserts, for example in Lapland, in the Aran isles and in Ukraine. Soft shoes lined with straw were considered to work better under wet conditions than the soled shoes known

[138] ÞÞ 1212.
[139] ÞÞ 1124.
[140] Hald, Margrethe, see earlier ref.
[141] Kaarma, Melanie, and Voolmaa, Aino, *Estonian Folk Costumes*, Tallinn 1981, pp. 58 and 83.

at the time. Special techniques and tools were used to choose and work the straw and place it in shoes. Wool was sometimes used as well, or wool mixed with straw.[142] In Norway, the Scandinavian Sami put juniper twigs in their shoes in the summer, and tree bark was used in northern Sweden during the warmest period of the year.[143] In Roman times, felted wool inserts were used in the legionnaires' sandals.[144]

Knitted inserts in soft shoes do not appear to have been used in other countries besides Iceland. The closest approach to the Icelandic soft shoes seems to have been the Faroese *skolingar*, which were knitted shoes with inserts consisting of double layers of felted knitted material that was sewn onto the bottom of the shoes. They were very useful in slippery conditions.[145] Modern shoes also have various kinds of insoles, made of leather, wool, and synthetic materials, that serve the same purpose as the inserts, "but they are naturally no better than the old knitted inserts," said Guðlaug Sveinbjörnsdóttir from Árnessýsla county (born 1927).[146]

In Iceland, hay was actually used if no inserts were available.[147] This was a last resort, however. Þórólfur Jónasson from Suður-Þingeyjarsýsla county (born 1892) remembers the vagabond "Gvendur Dúllari" who always had hay in his shoes, because according to him shoes lasted much longer "if you always walk on something soft."[148] Farmer- poet Páll Ólafsson saw hay in his wife's shoes and said:

Feginn vildi ég vera strá I'd like to be a wisp of hay
og visna í skónum þínum. and wither in your shoes.
Því léttast gengirðu eflaust á Because I know your step would be
yfirsjónum mínum.[149] ever so light on all my faults.

A wisp of hay was sometimes placed under the inserts in shoes if the weather turned very cold.[150] Wood shavings,[151] unspun horsehair,[152] and wool were used for the same purpose. If shoes proved too big, a wisp

---

142 Hald, Margrethe, see earlier ref.

143 Hald, Margrethe, see earlier ref.

144 Oakes, Alma, and Hill, Margot Hamilton, *Rural costume, Its origin and development in Western Europe and the British Isles,* London 1970, p. 148.

145 Guðrún Hadda Bjarnadóttir, "Heimilisiðnaðarbúðir", *Hugur og Hönd, Rit Heimilisiðnaðarfélags Íslands,* Reykjavík 1996.

146 ÞÞ 1540.

147 ÞÞ 7230.

148 ÞÞ 933.

149 The poem is quoted in ÞÞ 3818.

150 ÞÞ 947, 952.

151 ÞÞ 908.

152 ÞÞ 1069.

of hay might also be used.[153] Gray moss was put into shoes when walking through lava fields, if shoes had tears or holes in them.[154] If the weather was dry, stiff paper was sometimes used to cover a small hole.

> *Stúlkur, sjáið þið Steinunni stikla á pappírsskónum.*[155]
> Girls, look at Steinunn in her paper shoes watching her step.

Felt inserts made of discarded hats, for example, were put into the footwear worn on boats. Páll Pálsson from Norður-Ísafjarðarsýsla county (born 1883) said they "were considered soft under the foot and easy on sea-breeches".[156] Knitted inserts were most often used, however.

Uniquely Icelandic motif or intarsia knitting?

As discussed above, rose-pattern inserts in garter stitch use an old technique called motif knitting or intarsia, the oldest known example of which dates from the 14th century. This consists of Egyptian socks which combine Fair-Isle knitting and motif knitting.[157] But motif knitting does not seem to have been very common, at least not in the sense that it was used exclusively.

There is no mention of motif knitting or similar methods in histories of knitting in the Nordic countries.[158] So this skill did not come to Iceland via the Nordic countries any more than the techniques of knitting did in general. As discussed above, knitting was brought to Iceland by English, Dutch, or German merchants. It is therefore likely that motif knitting arrived here from the British Isles or northern Europe. Mary Thomas, an expert on knitting,[159] published a knitting manual in England in 1935, in which she explained this technique.[160] She calls it "geometric knitting" as it involves knitting geometric patterns in many colors. She takes the example of tartan socks from the Scottish highlands with a diamond pattern (called

---

[153] ÞÞ 932.

[154] ÞÞ 987 and 1009.

[155] ÞÞ 7401.

[156] ÞÞ 970.

[157] Rutt, Richard, see earlier ref., p. 39.

[158] For example, Pagoldh, Suzanne, *Nordic knitting*, London 1992.

[159] Regarding Mary Thomas, see for example Rutt, Richard, see earlier ref., p. 148.

[160] Thomas, Mary, see earlier ref., p. 111.

Argyle), knitted using intarsia technique.[161] But these socks were made using stocking stitch. I know of no tradition outside Iceland where intarsia was used with garter stitch, even though I have seen a few isolated examples of this.

Curator Íris Ólöf Sigurjónsdóttir[162] pointed out that different techniques, textures and patterns would not necessarily have emerged at the same time. Striped inserts are therefore probably older than rose-pattern inserts, as they use a simpler technique. As explained above, they were knitted in garter stitch for various reasons. Rose-pattern inserts may have emerged later when intarsia knitting was combined with garter stitch.

There are several examples of color knitting in Iceland. For example, during archaeological excavations in Reykholt, a small scrap of knitted material was found with a Fair-Isle border in two colors, which might date from the 17th century.[163] Elsa E. Guðjónsson discusses the possibility that the oldest known source on color knitting stems from 1695, the so-called corporal (communion cloth) with knitting in red and white.[164]

There are a few sources from the 18th and 19th centuries that mention decorative knitting (útprjón).[165] A Dutch physician named Martinet, who traveled around Iceland in 1794, describes Helga Jónsdóttir from Hálsasveit. She "had lost her sight due to smallpox, but she cut out, sewed, and did decorative knitting in several colors."[166] Sometimes, however, decorative knitting, útprjón, does not refer to color knitting but rather to lace knitting, gataprjón, as it does, for example, in the first manual on fine handiwork published in Iceland.[167] In my opinion, it is difficult to tell from the sources whether the reference is to Fair-Isle knitting or intarsia technique.

[161] Socks of this type are mass-produced today, for example, the so-called Burlington socks.

[162] Íris Ólöf Sigurjónsdóttir, the current curator of the district museum in Dalvík, in a conversation in January 2004.

[163] Elsa E. Guðjónsson, Fágæti úr fylgsnum jarðar, see earlier ref.

[164] Elsa E. Guðjónsson, Fágæti úr fylgsnum jarðar, see earlier ref.

[165] Háskóli Íslands, Orðabók Háskólans – ritmálsskrá, lexis.hi.is, 31/01/2004.

[166] Martinet, J.F., Edlis-útmálun Manneskjunnar, gjörd af Dr. Martinet. Translated from Danish by Sveinn Pálsson, Leirárgarðar 1798, p. 37.

[167] Þóra Pjetursdóttir, Jarþr. Jónsdóttir and Þóra Jónsdóttir, Leiðarvísir til að nema ýmsar kvenlegar hannyrðir, Reykjavík 1886, bls. 14.

Reproduction of a tablecloth with rose-pattern insert knitting by Guðlaug Jónsdóttir (1867-1939), owned by Fitjakot.

In some cases, decorative knitting definitively means intarsia technique, for example when talking about rose-pattern inserts.[168] I think it might also be a reference to intarsia when Eggert Ólafsson, who toured Iceland in the middle of the 18th century, talks about "the fine craft work practiced [...] by women [...] which consists of beautiful knitting with all kinds of images."[169]

The only thing we can be certain of is that intarsia technique was used in the 19th century in making rose-pattern inserts.[170] It is not known whether the technique was used for other types of clothing before the end of the 19th century. Rannveig Helgadóttir tells us about her great-grandmother, Guðlaug Jónsdóttir (1867-1939) who was "a housewife and mother of seven children in Fitjakot in Kjalarnes, a farm near Reykjavík. She handknitted tablecloths for her children and friends, late in the 19th century." These tablecloths were knitted with an old Icelandic method similar to intarsia technique. They were round, made of many small pieces decorated with eight-petal roses, flowerpots, and hourglasses. These parts were sewn together, and a knitted frill was sewn onto the outside edge. Copies have been made of some of these tablecloths.[171]

[168] Jónas Jónasson, see earlier ref.
[169] Eggert Ólafsson, *Ferðabók Eggerts Ólafssonar og Bjarna Pálssonar um ferðir þeirra á Íslandi árin 1752-1757*, Reykjavík, I, 1953, p. 124.
[170] Jónas Jónasson, see earlier ref.
[171] Rannveig Helgadóttir in a conversation in May 2005.

Rose-pattern knitted mittens: Textile Museum, Halldóra's room, Blönduós. They are done in stocking stitch rather than garter stitch. They won first prize in the Hlín competition, probably in 1924.

There are other examples of rose-pattern insert knitting in the 20th century, such as a wall-hanging in a frame from the beginning of the 20th century, which was very loosely knitted, with an intricate eight-petal rose[172] and two black seat cushions with a step rose in the middle.[173] Until about 1920, garments intended as Christmas presents, such as mittens, were often knitted with rose patterns.[174] We might mention as well a floor mat with squares

in two colors from 1928,[175] a blanket and a seat cushion made by Gróa Jakobsdóttir (1868-1953), with roses, wind roses and diamond shapes.[176] Sígríður Magnúsdóttir from Fljótshlíð (1855-1939) knitted shawls with stripes and eight-petal roses for her six daughters, and probably for her three daughters-in-law as well. According to her great-granddaughter, Steinunn J. Ásgeirsdóttir, rose-pattern insert knitting may have been more common in the south of Iceland than it was in the north.[177] Steinunn made a copy of one of these shawls, and the pattern was published in the magazine *Hugur og Hönd*, in 2005.[178]

Wall-hanging on a frame with an intricate eight-petal rose, early 20th century: Textile Museum, Halldóra's room, Blönduós.

[172] This rose might be a uniquely Icelandic motif, see Elsa E. Guðjónsson, *Íslenskur útsaumur,* Reykjavík 1985, pp. 33 and 34.
[173] Wall-hanging and seat cushions: Textile Museum, Halldóra's room, Blönduós.
[174] ÞÞ 3740.
[175] Rug described in Hlín, Reykjavík 1958, p. 157.
[176] Rug and seat cushions: Skógar.District Museum.
[177] Steinunn J. Ásgeirssdóttir in a conversation in April 2005.
[178] Steinunn J. Ásgeirssdóttir, "Langamma mín og sjölin", *Hugur og Hönd, Rit Heimilisiðnaðarfélasg Íslands,* Reykjavík 2005.

Rose-pattern insert knitting has not often been seen in recent decades. The magazine Hugur og Hönd published patterns for inserts with rose motifs in 1968 and again in 1996.[179] Insert-making has been part of courses on making soft skin shoes held by the Icelandic Handcrafts Society. The society also offered a course in making inserts for the first time in the spring of 2005, but it was not held because too few people registered for it. I know of two examples of rose-pattern knitting being used in contemporary handiwork. In 1977, Auður Sveinsdóttir published a sweater pattern with garter stitch and insert roses in Hugur og Hönd.[180] Rannveig Helgadóttir uses her grandmother's tablecloths as inspiration for new design. She sells various kinds of handiwork, such as pin cushions and tablecloths under the brand Fitjakot.[181]

Uniquely Icelandic patterns?

The most common everyday patterns were stripes. There may not be much to say about stripes as a motif, as they are the easiest way to decorate knitted material. They are certainly a very ancient knitting pattern. The oldest known example of stripes in knitwear is seen in children's socks from the seventh century that were discovered in Egypt.[182]

Roses can be mentioned in second place. This basic pattern is probably the most widespread motif in textiles around the world. Eight-petal roses are the most common, also known as snowflakes, as well as eight-pointed stars in some countries. The pattern might be a Christian symbol referring to the star of Bethlehem. This motif spread as the Christian faith expanded and is found in countries with many different cultures.[183] The rose is also associated with Christianity and can symbolize life, the soul, the heart, or love. Its significance corresponds to that of the lotus flower in many places in Asia.[184]

[179] Margrét Jakobsdóttir "Rósaleppar", Hugur og Hönd, Rit Heimilisiðnaðarfélags Íslands, Reykjavík 1968 and again in 1996.

[180] Auður Sveinsdóttir "Garðaprjónuð peysa með ílepparósum", Hugur og Hönd, Rit Heimilisiðnaðarfélags Íslands, Reykjavík 1977, p. 18.

[181] Among other things, Fitjakot has produced a beautiful tablecloth, knitted with motifs that symbolize Iceland. One of them is owned by the Icelandic Parliament, the Althing, and the President of Iceland has presented several tablecloths to foreign visitors as gifts.

[182] This might be nalbinding (nálbragð) instead of actual knitting. Nalbinding, which might be the origin of knitting, can be very similar to knitting in terms of texture, and it has often been confused with knitting. Rutt, Richard, see earlier ref., p. 32.

[183] Lind, Vibeke, Knitting in the Nordic tradition, Copenhagen 1981.

[184] http://perso.libertysurf.fr/sylphe.

Inserts with rose pattern: Inga B. Árnadóttir (1), Helga Þórarinsdóttir (2), National Museum of Iceland, Ethnological Collections (3 and 5) and Sigríður Halldórsdóttir (4). The first two roses are four-petal roses. The last two roses have no particular name, but I would call them "diamond roses".

This pattern may also have spread due to the nature of the technique itself. Some patterns are easier to work with than others and will therefore be more popular. These patterns are often symmetrical. The eight-petal rose can be found in Greek embroidery, in the beadwork of the native peoples of America, and bark textiles in Fiji. The pattern is also common in Thailand, Norway, the Shetland Islands,[185] and Azerbaijan,[186] and last but not least, in Iceland. But the Icelandic eight-petal rose does not seem to have had any particular significance; it was simply considered decorative.[187] The rose patterns can be of various types, such as step roses, wind roses or hammer roses, with either four or eight petals. The National Museum's Ethnological Collections Survey 12 and Icelandic Folk Customs (Íslenzkir þjóðhættir, Jónas Jónasson, see earlier reference) mention six-petal roses. I have never seen that pattern in knitting,

[185] McGregor, Sheila, The complete book of traditional Fair Isle knitting, London 1981.

[186] Heylen, John, The John Heylen Collection, place of publishing not mentioned.

[187] Birna Geirfinnsdóttir, Áttablaðarósin, BA thesis for the Iceland Academy of the Arts, advisor Guðrún Gunnarsdóttir, February 2006.

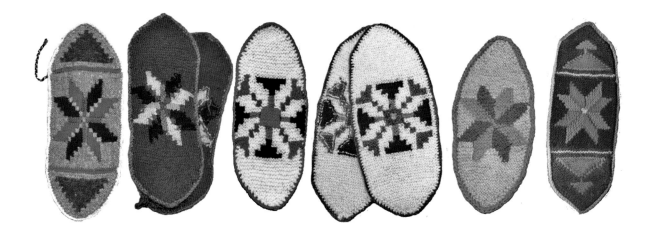

Inserts with step roses: National Museum of Iceland, Ethnological Collections (1 and 2), with hammer roses: National Museum of Iceland, Ethnological Collections (3) and Icelandic Handcrafts Society (4) and with wind roses: National Museum of Iceland, Ethnological Collections (5) and Elsa E. Guðjónsson (6.).

and I doubt it exists, as the complexity would make it difficult to execute. This might be a mistake in terminology or an incorrect memory.

Step roses (*stigarósir*) are eight-petal roses with an X-shape in the middle, which looks like two flights of stairs that meet in the middle. Hammer roses (*hamarrósir*)[188] were not very common in Iceland.[189] They consisted of eight arms with a hammer on the end of each arm. Wind roses (*vindrósir*) symbolize the mariner's compass and show the four cardinal directions and the wind directions between them (northeast, northwest, southeast, etc.). Wind roses are a very common pattern around the world.

---

[188] In Elsa Guðjónsson's article ("Um prjón á Íslandi", *Hugur og Hönd, Rit Heimilisiðnaðarfélags Íslands*, Reykjavík 1985), the names *hamarrós* and *högnakylfa* have been inverted in the picture captions. Elsa Guðjónsson corrected this mistake in a conversation with me in May 2005.

[189] Halldóra Bjarnadóttir, see earlier ref., p.184.

Checked inserts: National Museum of Iceland, Ethnological Collections (1 and 2) and diamond-pattern inserts: Textile Museum, Halldóra's room, Blönduós (3) and Skógar District Museum (4 and 5).

Aside from roses, diamond and checked patterns were the most common motifs in inserts. Diamonds and checks are patterns known around the world. They refer to the number four, which has many symbolic meanings, such as the four elements, the four seasons, the four cardinal directions, the four evangelists.[190] One large diamond in the middle was the simplest pattern for inserts, but there were other more complicated versions using diamond shapes. Checked inserts might have four checks in the middle and two in each tip.

[190] http://zan.zoom.free.fr/symbol.

Inserts with hourglass motif: National Museum of Iceland, Ethnological Collections (1 and 3), Árbæjarsafn, Reykjavík (2 and 5) and Dalvík District Museum (4).

Another pattern seen in inserts is the hourglass. This is a well-known symbol for the passage of time. A stylised hourglass that is very similar to those seen in Icelandic inserts is known from Faroese patterns.[191]

[191] Debes, Hans M., *Føroysk Bindingarmynstur, Føroysk heimavirki*, Tórshavn 1969.

Inserts with flowerpot motif: Skógar District Museum (1 and 4), Textile Museum, Halldóra's room, Blönduós (2), National Museum of Iceland, Ethnological Collections (3) and Icelandic Handcrafts Society (5).

Some inserts also show a stylized flowerpot. This motif is well known from embroidery pattern books and has been described as a symbol of friendship and love.[192] But the way it is stylized in Icelandic patterns is unusual. I have seen similar designs on the arms of knitted sweaters from Amager in Denmark. Sheila MacGregor, an American expert on knitting said that this pattern is unique in Denmark and attributes it to the community of Dutch immigrants in Amager.[193] In Iceland the pattern is usually more complicated and more worked, for example in cross-stitch on rose-pattern mittens.[194]

[192] http://www.needleworksamplers.com.

[193] McGregor, Sheila, *The complete book of traditional fair isle knitting,* London 1981.

[194] Elísabet Steinunn Jóhannsdóttir, *Skagfirskir rósavettlingar,* Sauðárkrókur 2003.

Inserts with spiked mace motif: National Museum of Iceland, Ethnological Collections (1, 4, 5), Icelandic Handcrafts Society (2) and Skógar District Museum, (3).

The spiked mace (*högnakylfa*)[195] is perhaps the only pattern seen in inserts that has no direct equivalent in other countries. The pattern is X-shaped, consisting of five rhombi, one in the middle and four in the corners. Each rhombus is divided into four triangles. The *högnakylfa* was a weapon, as seen from the following reference: *Það voru hreint ekki mennskir menn allt saman, heldur tröll og jötnar með járnása og Högnakylfur í höndum, sem öskrandi og beljandi geystust þar fram til orrustu.*[196] (They were not human at all, but rather trolls and giants carrying iron shafts and spiked maces, who hurled themselves, screaming and roaring, into the fray). The name of the weapon may have been derived from the man's name Högni, which by the way is the definition of a male cat. *Högnakylfa* was also the name of a game popular among mariners, a three-dimensional puzzle which involved assembling triangular shapes (spikes) out of many pieces.[197]

[195] See footnote 188.

[196] Árni Bjarnarson, *Að vestan I-IV, Þjóðsögur og sagnir,* Akureyri 1949-1955, I, p. 19.

[197] Lúðvík Kristjánsson, *Íslenskir sjávarhættir I-V,* Reykjavík 1980-1986, p. 205-206. There is a picture of the puzzle there.

As in the case of other kinds of handiwork, knitting patterns were often passed on from one generation to the next.[198] Insert patterns were no exception. "Some women changed the patterns they were given and even invented new ones," said Kristján G. Þorvaldsson from Vestur-Ísafjarðarsýsla county (born 1881).[199] Some examples of innovations were Christmas trees,[200] oak trees, or claw knitting (*klóaprjón*), the latter pattern being taken from foreign knitting patterns.[201] Sometimes the year inserts were knitted was used instead of a pattern.

And finally, some knitted inserts had crosses in the tips, in the middle of the rose, or at the top of a flowerpot. Crosses were sometimes knitted on seamen's mittens as protection against evil.[202]

But some people did not like the

Inserts with unconventional designs: Árbæjarsafn, Reykjavík (1 and 2) and Textile Museum, Halldóra's room, Blönduós (3-6).

[198] Dawson, Pam, *Traditional Island Knitting,* Tunbridge Wells 1988, p. 108.

[199] ÞÞ 930.

[200] ÞÞ 952.

[201] ÞÞ 981.

[202] Sigríður Halldórsdóttir, weaving teacher, former principal of the Handicrafts School in Reykjavík, in a conversation in January 2004.

idea of knitting crosses into inserts.[203] "It was considered unchristian to walk on the symbol of the faith," said Jónína Jóhannsdóttir from Rangárvallasýsla county (born 1907).[204]

As described above, most of the motifs used in inserts, with the possible exception of the spiked mace, have some equivalent in other countries. Without entering into a discussion of what could be termed "particularly Icelandic" and what could not, I can say that these motifs are hardly uniquely Icelandic in terms of form.[205] But the use of a motif in one country can be unique in terms of the materials used, the texture, colors, or color combinations, to name just a few characteristics. White, knitted, eight-petal roses (or snowflakes) repeated on a red or black background are considered typically Norwegian, for example, and the same rose on a striped background in indigo, dark red, or yellow is typical of the Shetland Islands. The same eight-petal rose, alone on a one-color background, with two or four petals in different colors and a heart in another color, could be called typically Icelandic, especially if the rose is knitted using garter stitch. Some people probably consider inserts that are knitted from Icelandic wool or yarn, colored using dyes made from Icelandic plants or left in the natural colors of the wool, to be more Icelandic than others, and I would concur with that point of view. The spiked mace pattern is the insert motif that has no direct equivalent elsewhere and could justifiably be called uniquely Icelandic. But even though I cannot present any particular argument to support my opinion, this pattern has never seemed particularly Icelandic to me. It is mainly the variety of colors used in this country, the unique color combinations, and the use of garter stitch combined with intarsia technique that makes Icelandic insert patterns unique.

Conclusion

Icelandic inserts display a mixture of techniques, materials, motifs/patterns, colors, and color combinations that distinguish them from those known from other countries. The techniques used in making inserts and

[203] Often noted in ÞÞ.
[204] ÞÞ 947.
[205] Icelandic nationality will not be discussed here. On this subject, see Guðmundur Hálfdanarson, *Íslenska þjóðríkið – uppruni og endimörk*, Reykjavík 2001, p. 171 etc.

their textures were not common in Europe, and as far as I know, the use of garter stitch with intarsia knitting is unknown outside Iceland. So it could be said that both inserts and rose-pattern insert knitting are a particularly Icelandic phenomenon.

The knitting of rose-pattern inserts has now disappeared as a living craft. And of course it is highly unlikely that we will ever revert to a time when people sit on the edge of their beds in the evening and knit inserts. But we can show our respect for old traditions by reinterpreting them and continuing to use them in new and changed circumstances. Inserts and insert-motifs can serve as important sources of ideas for developing new forms of knitting that can be called uniquely Icelandic. It would therefore be a great loss for Icelandic knitting if the techniques used in making inserts and rose-pattern insert knitting were to be lost. It is my hope that this book will help prevent such an unfortunate development.

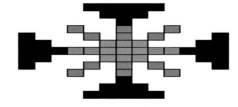

Bibliography

Written sources

Auður Sveinsdóttir, "Garðaprjónuð peysa með ílepparósum", *Hugur og Hönd, Rit Heimilisiðnaðarfélags Íslands*, Reykjavík 1977

Árni Bjarnarson, *Að vestan I-IV, Þjóðsögur og sagnir*, Akureyri 1949-1955

Birna Geirfinnsdóttir, *Áttablaðarósin*, BA thesis for the Iceland Academy of the Arts, advisor Guðrún Gunnarsdóttir, February 2006

Dawson, Pam, *Traditional Island Knitting*, Tunbridge Wells 1988

Debes, Hans M., *Føroysk Bindingarmynstur*, Þórshöfn 1969

Eggert Ólafsson, *Ferðabók Eggerts Ólafssonar og Bjarna Pálssonar um ferðir þeirra á Íslandi árin 1752-1757*, Reykjavík, I, 1953

Elsa E. Guðjónsson, "Fágæti úr fylgsnum jarðar, Fornleifar í þágu textíl- og búningarannsókna", *Skírnir: ný tíðindi hins íslenzka bókmenntafélags*, 1992, 166 (vor)

Elsa E. Guðjónsson, *Íslenskur útsaumur*, Reykjavík 1985

Elsa E. Guðjónsson, *Prjón á Íslandi*, Reykjavík 1990

Elsa E. Guðjónsson, "Um prjón á Íslandi", *Hugur og Hönd, Rit Heimilisiðnaðarfélags Íslands*, Reykjavík 1985

Elísabet Steinunn Jóhannsdóttir, *Skagfirskir rósavettlingar*, Sauðárkrókur 2003

Fríður Ólafsdóttir, *Íslensk karlmannaföt 1740-1850*, Reykjavík 1999

Gibson-Roberts, Priscilla A., *Knitting in the old way*, Colorado 1985

Guðmundur Erlendsson, *Grobbions rímur séra Guðmundar Erlendssonar*, XIII 1-3 Reykjavík 1915-16-33, 47v, 17 fm

Guðmundur Hálfdanarson, *Íslenska þjóðríkið – uppruni og endimörk*, Reykjavík 2001

Guðmundur Þorsteinsson frá Lundi, *Horfnir starfshættir og leiftur frá liðnum öldum*, Reykjavík 1975

Guðrún Hadda Bjarnadóttir, "Heimilisiðnaðarbúðir", *Hugur og Hönd, Rit Heimilisiðnaðarfélags Íslands*, Reykjavík 1996

Hald, Margrethe, *Primitive shoes, An Archeological-Ethnological Study Based upon Shoe Finds from the Jutland peninsula*, Copenhagen 1972

Halldóra Bjarnadóttir, *Vefnaður á íslenskum heimilum*, Reykjavík 1966

Harte N.B. and Ponting K.G., *Cloth and Clothing in Medieval Europe, Essays in memory of Professor E.M. Carus-Wilson*, London 1983

Háskóli Íslands, *Orðabók Háskólans – ritmálsskrá*, lexis.hi.is, 31/01/2004

Heylen, John, *The John Heylen Collection*, place of publication and date not given

Hlín, *Gólfábreiða*, Reykjavík 1958

Hulda Á. Stefánsdóttir, "Um íslenskan klæðnað", *Hugur og Hönd, Rit Heimilisiðnaðarfélags Íslands*, Reykjavík 1979

Inga Lárusdóttir, *Vefnaður, prjón og saumur*, Iðnsaga íslands II, Reykjavík 1943

Jón Helgason and Stefán Einarsson, *Breiðdæla: Drög til sögu Breiðdals*, Reykjavík 1948

Jón J. Aðils, *Einokunarverzlun Dana á Íslandi 1602-1787*, Reykjavík 1971

Jón G. Friðjónsson, *Mergur málsins - Íslensk orðatiltæki, uppruni, saga og notkun*, Reykjavík 1993

Jónas Jónasson, *Íslenzkir þjóðhættir*, Reykjavík 1961

Kaarma, Melanie, and Voolmaa, Aino, *Estonian Folk Costumes*, Tallinn 1981

Lind, Vibeke, *Knitting in the Nordic tradition*, Kaupmannahöfn 1981

Lúðvík Kristjánsson, *Íslenskir sjávarhættir I-V*, Reykjavík 1980-1986

McGregor, Sheila, *The complete book of traditional Fair Isle knitting*, London 1981

McGregor, Sheila, *The complete book of traditional Scandinavian knitting*, New York 1984

Margrét Jakobsdóttir, "Rósaleppar", *Hugur og Hönd, Rit Heimilisiðnaðarfélags Íslands*, Reykavík 1968

Margrét Jakobsdóttir, "Rósaleppar", *Hugur og Hönd, Rit Heimilisiðnaðarfélags Íslands*, Reykjavík 1996

Martinet, J.F., *Edlis-útmálun Manneskjunnar, gjørd af Dr. Martinet.* Translated from Danish by Sveinn Pálsson, Leirárgarðar 1798

Oakes, Alma, and Hill, Margot Hamilton, *Rural costume, Its origin and development in Western Europe and the British Isles,* London 1970

Pagoldh, Suzanne, *Nordic knitting,* London 1992

Rutt, Richard, *A history of hand-knitting,* London 2003
Ryall, Pierre, *Le tissage à la main,* Montbéliard, year of publication not given

Sigríður Halldórsdóttir, "Slyngdir leppar", *Hugur og Hönd, Rit Heimilisiðnaðarfélags Íslands,* Reykjavík 1973

Steinunn J. Ásgeirsdóttir, "Langamma mín og sjölin", *Hugur og Hönd, Rit Heimilisiðnaðarfélags Íslands,* Reykjavík 2005

Thomas, Mary, *Mary Thomas's Knitting Book,* New York 1938

Þorkell Jóhannesson, *Ullariðnaður, Iðnsaga íslands II,* Reykjavík 1943
Þjóðskjalasafn Íslands, Bbps, Copenhagen 1878, AII 10, 53r (1642), AII 8, 478 (1672) og AII 7, 156 (1662)
Þóra Pjetursdóttir, Jarþr. Jónsdóttir and Þóra Jónsdóttir, *Leiðarvísir til að nema ýmsar kvenlegar hannyrðir,* Reykjavík 1886
Þórdís Kristleifsdóttir, "Rósaleppaprjón – séríslenskt myndprjón?", *Hugur og Hönd, Rit Heimilisiðnaðarfélags Íslands,* Reykjavík 1996

Unpublished source material in the National Museum of Iceland, Ethnological Collections

Replies to Survey 12, Shoemaking, 1964. Sources quoted – sex, year of birth and places of reference:

ÞÞ 908 male born 1884, Meðalland, Vestur-Skaftafellssýsla

ÞÞ 913 male born 1902, Hveragerðishreppur, Árnessýsla

ÞÞ 915 male born 1919, Norður-Múlasýsla

ÞÞ 917 male born 1887, Biskupstungnahreppur, Árnessýsla

ÞÞ 924 male born 1882, Álftaver, Vestur-Skaftafellssýsla

ÞÞ 928 – 940 male born 1881, Fljótsdalshérað, Múlasýsla

ÞÞ 929 male born 1900, Miðfjörður, Vestur-Húnavatnssýsla

ÞÞ 930 male born 1881, Súgandafjörður, Vestur-Ísafjarðarsýsla

ÞÞ 932 male born 1905, Kelduhverfi, Norður-Þingeyjarsýsla

ÞÞ 933 male born 1892, Aðaldælahreppur, Suður-Þingeyjarsýsla

ÞÞ 936 male born 1884, Skaftafellssýsla

ÞÞ 940 male born 1881, Fellahreppur, Norður-Múlasýsla

ÞÞ 945 male born 1901, Borgarfjörður eystri, Úthérað, Vopnafjörður, Norður-Múlasýsla

ÞÞ 946 male born 1896, Laxárdalur í Dölum

ÞÞ 947 female born 1907, Rangárvallasýsla

ÞÞ 949 male born 1895, Hurðarbak, Hvalfjarðarstrandarhreppur, Borgarfjarðarsýsla

ÞÞ 951 male born 1889, Rangárvallasýsla

ÞÞ 952 male born 1889, Álftaneshreppur, Vestur-Mýrasýsla

ÞÞ 955 female born 1886, Vestur-Ísafjarðarsýsla

ÞÞ 964 female born 1891, Árnessýsla and Rangárvallasýsla

ÞÞ 970 male born 1883, Hnífsdalur, Norður-Ísafjarðarsýsla

ÞÞ 971 male born 1895, Austur-Barðastrandarsýsla

ÞÞ 973 female born 1902, Sléttuhreppur, Norður-Ísafjarðarsýsla

ÞÞ 976 female born 1907, Flateyjarhreppur, Austur-Barðastrandarsýsla

ÞÞ 979 female born 1893, Árnessýsla

ÞÞ 981 male born 1895, Suður-Þingeyjarsýsla

ÞÞ 985 female born 1885, Breiðdalshreppur, Suður-Múlasýsla

ÞÞ 987 male born 1900, Hnappadalssýsla

ÞÞ 989 male born 1887, Norður-Ísafjarðarsýsla

ÞÞ 990 male born 1901, Svalbarðsstrandarhreppur, Suður-Þingeyjarsýsla

ÞÞ 991 male born 1891, Mið- and Úthérað, Múlasýsla

ÞÞ 993 males born 1892 and 1932, Reykjarfjarðarhreppur, Norður-Ísafjarðarsýsla

ÞÞ 999 male born 1898, Ölfus, Árnessýsla

ÞÞ 1000 male born 1884, Skagafjörður, Skagafjarðarsýsla.

ÞÞ 1001 male born 1918, Skagafjarðarsýsla and Húnavatnssýsla

ÞÞ 1002 female born 1895, Norður-Þingeyjarsýsla and Múlasýsla

ÞÞ 1006 male born 1902, Skagafjarðarsýsla and Eyjafjarðarsýsla

ÞÞ 1007 male born 1918, Austur-Húnavatnssýsla

ÞÞ 1009 male born 1892, Suður-Þingeyjarsýsla

ÞÞ 1018 female born 1905, Skagafjörður, Skagafjarðarsýsla.

ÞÞ 1039 female born 1875, Vestur-Eyjafjallasveit, Rangárvallasýsla

ÞÞ 1040 male born 1908, Mosfellssveit and Hafnarfjörður, Árnessýsla

ÞÞ 1059 male born 1898, Suður-Dölum

ÞÞ 1069 female born 1900, Bæjarhreppur and Hrútafjörður, Strandasýsla

ÞÞ 1071 male born 1896, Áshreppur, west of Blanda, Austur-Húnavatnssýsla

ÞÞ 1082 male born 1858, Kelduhverfi and Axarfjörður, Norður-Þingeyjarsýsla

ÞÞ 1124 male born 1908, Hreppar, Árnessýsla

ÞÞ 1146 male born 1884, Nesjasveit, Austur-Skaftafellssýsla

ÞÞ 1210 female born 1904, Reykhólasveit, Austur-Barðastrandarsýsla

ÞÞ 1212 male born 1895, Kolbeinsstaðahreppur, Hnappadalssýsla

ÞÞ 1410 male born 1928, Fljótsdalshérað, Múlasýsla

ÞÞ 1540 female born 1927, Hraungerðishreppur, Árnessýsla

ÞÞ 1719 male born 1893, Barðaströnd, Vestur-Barðastrandarsýsla

ÞÞ 3818 male born 1900, Hjaltastaðahreppur, Norður-Múlasýsla

ÞÞ 7215 female born 1898, Öxnadalur, Eyjafjarðarsýsla

ÞÞ 7218 female born 1903, Fnjóskadalur, Suður-Þingeyjarsýsla

ÞÞ 7225 female born 1900, Tjörnes, Suður-Þingeyjarsýsla

ÞÞ 7229 female born 1901, Núpasveit, Slétta, Norður-Þingeyjarsýsla

ÞÞ 7230 female born 1903, Aðaldalur, Köldukinn, Suður-Þingeyjarsýsla

ÞÞ 7231 female born 1910, Aðaldalur, Húsavík, Suður-Þingeyjarsýsla

ÞÞ 7232 females born 1905 and 1893, Hólsfjöll, Norður-Þingeyjarsýsla

ÞÞ 7233 female born 1906, Jökulsárhlíð, Vopnafjörður, Norður-Múlasýsla

ÞÞ 7234 female born 1911, Fljót, Svarfaðardalur, Skagafjarðarsýsla and Eyjafjarðarsýsla

ÞÞ 7254 female born 1902, Biskupstungur, Flói, Vestmannaeyjar, Árnes- and Rangárvallasýsla

ÞÞ 7256 female born 1910, Vestmannaeyjar, Rangárvallasýsla

ÞÞ 7257 female born 1910, Vestmannaeyjar, Rangárvallasýsla

ÞÞ 7258 female born 1911, Hérað and Breiðdalur, Suður-Múlasýsla

ÞÞ 7260 female born 1903, Tjörnes, Suður-Þingeyjarsýsla

ÞÞ 7401 female born 1901, Árneshreppur, Strandasýsla

Replies to Survey 31, Holidays and special occasions, 1975. Sources quoted – sex, year of birth and places of reference:

ÞÞ 3740, male born 1901, Suður-Þingeyjarsýsla

ÞÞ 4200 female born 1910, Aðaldalur and Langanes, Þingeyjarsýsla

Electronic sources

For the symbolic meaning of the rose: www.perso.libertysurf.fr/sylphe, February 2004

For the meaning of the flowerpot motif: www.zan.zoom.free.fr/symbol, February 2004

For the meaning of the number four: www.shakespearespeddler.com/symbol, May 2006

Oral sources

Áslaug Sverrisdóttir, curator, Árbær Museum, January 2004

Elsa E. Guðjónsson, former curator, Textile and costume department of the National Museum of Iceland, January 2004 and May 2005

Helga Þórarinsdóttir, handiwork teacher and folk dance instructor, April 2005

Íris Ólöf Sigurjónsdóttir, curator, Dalvík district museum, January 2004

Olga Hallgrímsdóttir, September 2003

Rannveig Helgadóttir, Fitjakot, May 2005

Sigríður Halldórsdóttir, weaving teacher, former principal of the Handicrafts School in Reykjavík, January 2004

Steinunn Ásgeirsdóttir, April 2005

Photographs by Hélène Magnússon: photographs of inserts and rose-pattern insert knitting taken during the period 1999-2006, belonging to:

Árbær Museum, Reykjavík

Dalvík District Museum (Hvolur)

Glaumbær District Museum

Skógar District Museum

Suður-Þingeyinga District Museum (Branches in Húsavík and Grenjaðarstaðir)

Elsa E. Guðjónsson

Erla Þórarinsdóttir

Guðrún Egilsdóttir

Textile Museum, Halldóra's room, Blönduós

Icelandic Handcrafts Society, Reykjavík

Helga Þórarinsdóttir

Inga B. Árnadóttir

Akureyri Museum

Rannveig Helgadóttir, Fitjakot, Hafnarfjörður

Sigríður Halldórsdóttir

Steinunn Ásgeirsdóttir

Svava Björnsdóttir

Þingborg, Handicraft Association, Selfoss

National Museum of Iceland, Ethnological Collections

Rose-pattern knitting, new ideas

Prjóna átti píkan ein
peysu fyrir ungan svein
ólaglega að því fór
aldrei var hún nógu stór.

ÞÞ 955

The lass was set a simple task,
To knit a sweater for the lad,
But she had little luck in this,
For it turned out far too small.

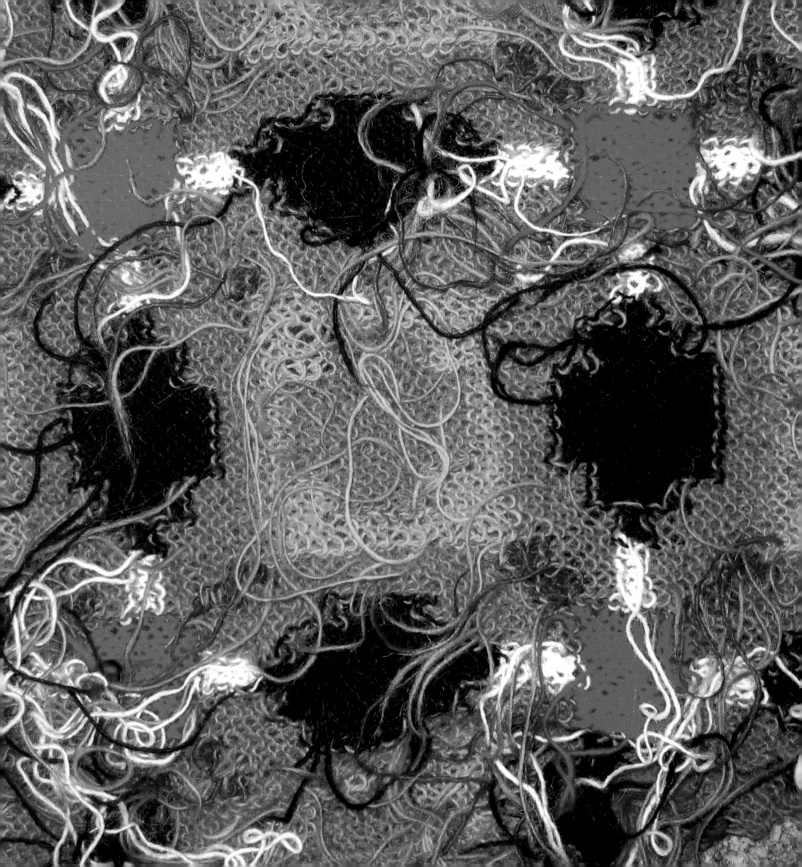

Techniques

Rose-pattern insert knitting

Rose-pattern insert knitting is worked in the same way as regular motif or intarsia knitting.

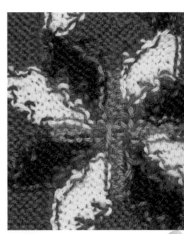

It is easier to follow the pattern when knitting in garter stitch because this is done the same way whether knitting on the wrong side or on the right side.

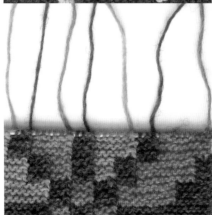

Each block of color requires a separate bobbin or ball of yarn. It is a good idea to keep the bobbins close the needles to avoid tangling the yarn.

Home-made ball of yarn.

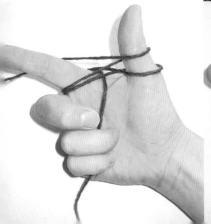

Plastic bag with rubber band.

Small clothes-pin.

Card for yarn.

When the block of color is small, the length of yarn can simply be left loose.

When joining in a new color, the yarn is drawn over the yarn that has been used so far.

Right side.

Wrong side.

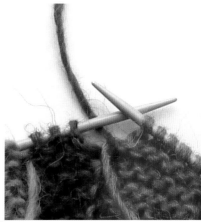

The new yarn must be on the right side of the color block to be knitted. As the pattern moves to the left, it is knitted-in (shown here on the wrong side).

When the pattern moves to the right, the yarn is left lying across the wrong side, then knitted-in (shown here on the wrong side).

It is a good idea to knit in or darn in loose ends regularly while working.

In some cases, in order to avoid unnecessary loose ends, begin at the center stitch and work the ends individually in both directions.

In order to determine the length of yarn needed, when working a small block of color, wind the yarn as many times around the needle as the number of stitches required.

In some cases it is possible to work a piece using both intarsia and Fair Isle knitting technique. For instance, the pattern is knitted using intarsia technique while the main color is knitted along the whole way.

In some cases garter stitch is worked along with Fair Isle knitting technique.

Swiss darning

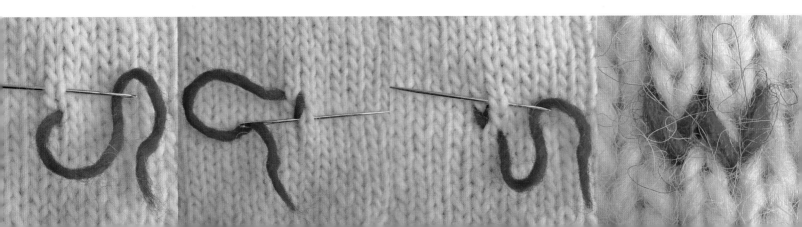

Band-weave edging (*Slynging*)

Wind the warp using six to eight threads of yarn, alternating dark and light colors. The length of the warp is 3-4 times the circumference of the insert.

Separate dark and light threads. Bring the threads alternately up and down to form the weft, then thread it.

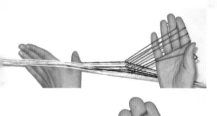

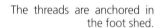

The threads are anchored in the foot shed.

The right foot is slipped into the foot shed. The shed is opened and the weft is drawn through the shed.

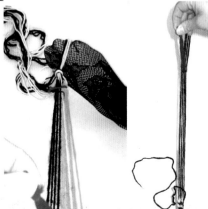

Change sheds. The weft is drawn through the shed. Continue weaving until a short length of band is formed.

Now begin the process of slynging, i.e. simultaneously weaving and attaching the band to the insert as follows: the needle is slipped through the shed and drawn up through the material.

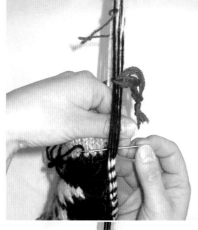 

Change sheds.

The needle is slipped through the shed and drawn up through the material.

Change sheds.

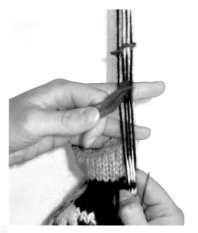

Continue.

Right side.

Wrong side.

Knitting patterns

Hammer rose vest
p. 102
1

Hammer rose cardigan
p. 104
2

Step rose sweater
p. 106
3

Flowerpot sweater
p. 108
4

Eight-petal rose sweater
p. 110
5

A second eight-petal rose
sweater
p. 111
6

Rose-pattern sweater
p. 113
7

Spiked mace sweater
p. 115
8

My Icelandic sweater
and mittens
p. 116
9

19 Flowerpot sweater with hood — p. 143

20 Delicate mittens — p. 146

21 Rose-pattern mittens and matching beret — p. 148

22 Cap, beret, bag and mittens — p. 150

23 Child's cap and mittens — p. 153

24 Narrow scarf with roses — p. 155

25 Narrow scarf with flowerpots — p. 157

26 Band-weave edged potholders — p. 158

*Fimm á milli fyrsta sinn
þú ferð að prjóna.
Vertu iðin verk að prjóna
varastu að glápa og góna.*
ÞÞ 979.

Five on hand the first time
You'll be knitting now.
Concentrate on the work at hand
Don't go casting looks around.

st, sts = stitch, stitches
k = knit stitch
p = purl stitch
mm = millimeter
cm = centimeter
sc = single crochet
dc = double crochet
N.B. = Nota Bene (note well)
approx. = approximately
S (M) L = Small (Medium) Large

The garments were made using the following yarns:
- Loðband - einband from Ístex: 100 % new Icelandic wool, 50 gr balls. 50 gr equal approx. 225 meters.
- Álafoss lopi from Ístex: 100 % new Icelandic wool, 100 gr balls. 100 gr equal approx. 100 meters.
- Létt-lopi from Ístex: 100 % new Icelandic wool, 50 gr balls. 50 gr equal approx. 100 meters.
- Kambgarn from Ístex: 100 % new merino wool, 50 gr balls. 50 gr equal approx. 150 meters.
- Kitten Mohair from Sandnes Garn: 30% mohair, 20% wool, 50% courtelle, 50 gr balls. 50 gr equal approx. 165 meters.

All yarn used in these patterns can be ordered from the Handknitting Association of Iceland, Skólavörðustíg 19, 101 Reykjavík, Iceland
Telephone: +354 5521890
Fax: +354 5521912
handknit@handknit.is
www.handknit.is

Yarn suppliers outside Iceland:
Ístex, Póstholf 140, 270 Mosfellsbær
Telephone: +354 5666300
Fax: +354 5667330
istex@istex.is
www.istex.is

1 Hammer rose vest

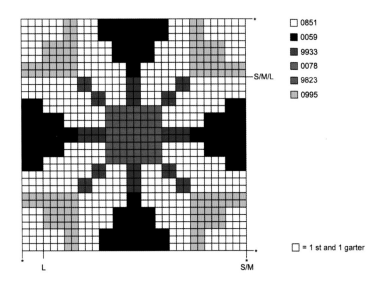

0851
0059
9933
0078
9823
0995

S/M/L

□ = 1 st and 1 garter

L   S/M

Inserts: National Museum of Iceland, Ethnological Collections.

Size: S (M) L
Width: approx. 102 (112) 120 cm
Length: approx. 54 (55) 58 cm
Materials: Loðband - einband from Ístex
- white 0851, 3 (3) 4 balls
- black 0059, 2 balls
- violet 9933, 1 ball
- bright red 0078, 1 ball
- green 9823, 1 ball
- yellow 0995, 1 ball
Needles: 4 (4½) 4½ mm needles, 3 mm crochet hook

Tension: 10 x 10 cm using garter stitch and intarsia technique on 4 (4½) mm needles equal 19 (18) sts and 21 (19) garters.

□ = 1 st and 1 garter

Knitting method: The vest is knitted back and forth using garter stitch and intarsia technique.

Garter stitch: 1 garter = 2 rows k worked back and forth

Picot edging: 1st row: crochet 1 slip st in the edge, *1 sc, repeat from*. 2nd row: crochet 1 slip st and then *1 picot (3 chain sts, 1 slip st in second chain st, 1 slip st in first chain st), pass over 2 sts, 1 sc in next st, repeat from*.

Front: Cast on 96 (96)102 sts using 4 (4½) 4½ mm needles and white yarn. Knit pattern in garter st, beginning at the appropriate mark according to size. Repeat pattern from *-* to end of row and also from *-* upward. N.B.: □ = 1 st and 1 garter. When the front measures approx. 31 (32) 33 cm, shape armholes by casting off 6 sts on each side and continue decreasing 1 st in each garter five times and 1 st in every fifth garter three times. When the front measures approx. 47 (48) 51 cm, cast off for the neck opening 14 sts in the middle, then on each side 2 sts in each garter (three) four times. Knit each shoulder individually. When the front measures approx. 53 (54) 57 cm, shape shoulder by casting off 6 (6) 7 sts in each garter twice, then remaining sts.

Back: Knit the back like the front but don't start casting off for the neck opening until the back measures approx. 50 (51) 54 cm, then cast off 24 sts in the middle and on each side 1 st in each garter four times. Knit each shoulder individually. When the back measures approx. 53 (54) 57 cm, shape shoulder as on front.

Finishing: Sew shoulder seams. Sew side seams until there are 4 (4) 5 cm left from the lower edge (slit). Crochet a picot edging using 3 mm hook and white yarn at the lower edge, around the armholes and around the neck opening. Darn in loose ends.

2 Hammer rose cardigan

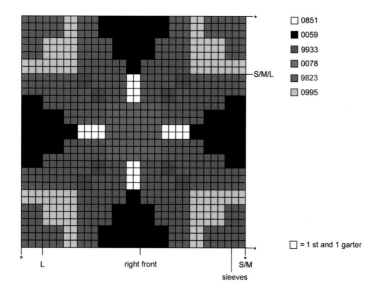

0851
0059
9933
0078
9823
0995

S/M/L

☐ = 1 st and 1 garter

*
L   right front   S/M
                              sleeves

Size: S (M) L
Width: approx. 102 (112) 120 cm
Length: approx. 54 (55) 58 cm
Sleeve length to armhole: approx. 40 (41) 42 cm
Materials: Loðband - einband from Ístex
- white 0851, 1 ball
- black 0059, 3 balls
- violet 9933, 1 ball
- bright red 0078, 3 balls
- green 9823, 5 (5) 6 balls
- yellow 0995, 3 balls
6 (6) 7 green buttons

Needles: 4 (4½) 4½ mm needles, 3 mm crochet hook
Tension: 10 x 10 cm using garter stitch and intarsia technique on 4 (4½) mm needles equal 19 (18) sts and 21 (19) garters.
□ = 1 st and 1 garter
Knitting method: The sweater is knitted back and forth using garter stitch and intarsia technique.
Garter stitch: 1 garter = 2 rows k worked back and forth
Edging: 1st row: crochet 1 slip st into edge, *1 sc, repeat from*. 2nd row: crochet 1 slip st, *1 small picot (2 chain sts, 1 slip st in first chain st), pass over 2 sts, 1 sc in next st, repeat from*.

Right front: Cast on 49 (49) 52 sts using 4 (4½) 4½ mm needles and green yarn. Knit 3 garters and then, continuing in garter st, knit pattern beginning at the appropriate mark according to size. N.B: □ = 1 st and 1 garter. Repeat pattern from *-* to end of row and also from *-* upward. When the front measures approx. 28 (30) 34 cm, shape armhole by casting off 6 sts on the left side and continue decreasing 1 st in each garter five times and then 1 st in every fifth garter three times. When the front measures approx. 48 (50) 54 cm, cast off on the right side for the neck opening 7 sts, then 2 sts in each garter three times and 1 st in every other garter three (three) four times. When the front measures approx. 54 (56) 60 cm, shape shoulder by casting off 6 (6) 7 sts in each garter twice, then remaining sts.
Left front: Knit the left front as a mirror image of the right front.
Back: Cast on 96 (96) 102 sts using 4 (4½) 4½ mm needles and green yarn. Knit 3 garters and then, continuing in garter st, knit pattern beginning at the appropriate mark according to size. When the back measures approx. 28 (30) 34 cm, shape armholes by casting off 6 sts on each side and continue decreasing 1 st in each garter five times, then 1 st in every fifth garter three times. When the back measures approx. 51 (53) 57 cm cast off for the neck opening 24 sts in the middle and then on each side 1 st in each garter four times. Knit each shoulder individually. When the back measures approx. 54 (56) 60 cm shape shoulder by casting off 6 sts in each garter twice (twice) three times, then remaining sts.
Sleeves: Cast on 60 (60) 60 sts using 4 (4½) 4½ mm needles and green yarn. Knit 3 garters and then continuing in garter st, knit pattern beginning at the appropriate mark according to size. Repeat pattern from*-* to end of row and also from *-* upward. When the sleeve

measures approx. 40 (41) 42 cm, shape armhole by casting off 6 sts on each side, then 1 st in each garter, five times and 1 st in every fifth garter three times. When the sleeve measures approx. 54 (55) 56 cm cast off 2 sts on each side in each garter three times. Cast off remaining sts.

Finishing: Sew shoulder seams. Sew sleeves into armholes. Sew side seams and underarm seams. Crochet a picot edging, using a 3 mm crochet hook and green yarn on the edge of the fronts and around the neck opening. Make six (six) seven buttonholes on the right front by crocheting the second row as follows: **crochet 1 chain st, 1 small picot, 1 chain st, pass over 2 sts, *1 sc in next st, repeat six times from*, repeat six (six) seven times from**. Sew the buttons on the left front opposite the buttonholes. Darn in loose ends.

3 Step rose sweater

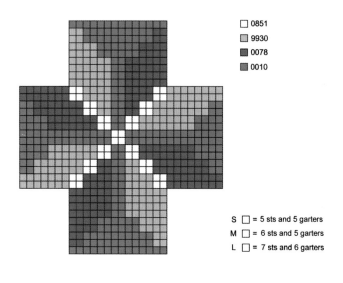

☐ 0851
▨ 9930
▨ 0078
▨ 0010

S ☐ = 5 sts and 5 garters
M ☐ = 6 sts and 5 garters
L ☐ = 7 sts and 6 garters

Inserts: Textile Museum, Halldóra's room, Blönduós.

Size: S (M) L
Width: approx. 85 (100) 115 cm
Length: approx. 46 (46) 54 cm
Materials: Loðband - einband from Ístex
- white 0851, 1 ball
- lavender 9930, 1 ball
- bright red 0078, 1 ball
- blue 0010, 2 (2) 3 balls
Needles: 4 mm and 4½ mm needles, 3 mm crochet hook
Tension: 10 x 10 cm in garter stitch on 4½ mm needles equal 17 sts and 20 garters.
S: □ = 5 sts and 5 garters
M: □ = 6 sts and 5 garters
L: □ = 7 sts and 6 garters
Knitting method: The sweater is knitted back and forth in one piece using garter stitch and intarsia technique.
Garter stitch: 1 garter = 2 rows k worked back and forth

Sweater: Cast on 70 (84) 98 sts using 4 mm needles and blue yarn. Knit 6 cm ribbing (k2, p1). Change to 4½ mm needles and knit pattern in garter st. N.B.: S: □ = 5 sts and 5 garters, M: □ = 6 sts and 5 garters, L: □ = 7 sts and 6 garters. Upon reaching the armhole, cast on 40 (48) 56 sts on each side for the sleeves. Cast off 50 (52) 54 sts in the middle at mid-pattern for the neck opening, then cast them back on in the next row. Upon reaching armhole again, cast off 40 (48) 56 sts on both sides. When the pattern is complete, change to 4 mm needles and knit 6 cm ribbing (k2, p1) with blue yarn. Cast off.

Finishing: Pick up 60 (62) 64 sts from the sleeves using 4 mm needles and blue yarn and knit 4 cm ribbing (k2, p1). Cast off. Sew side seams and underarm seams. Crochet an edging around the neck opening, using sc and 3 mm crochet hook as follows: 30 (36) 42 sts in the middle of the front and back with lavender yarn and 20 (16) 12 sts on each side with red yarn. Crochet 2 rows, break off yarn and darn in all loose ends.

4 Flowerpot sweater

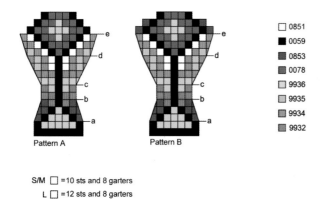

☐	0851
■	0059
▨	0853
▨	0078
▨	9936
▨	9935
▨	9934
▨	9932

Pattern A   Pattern B

S/M ☐ =10 sts and 8 garters
L ☐ =12 sts and 8 garters

Inserts: Textile Museum, Halldóra's room, Blönduós.

Size: S/M (L)
Width: approx. 82 (98) cm
Length to armhole: approx. 44 (44) cm
Sleeve length to armhole: approx. 47 (48) cm
Materials: Loðband - einband from Ístex
- white 0851, 1 ball
- acorn heather 0853, 1 ball
- bright red 0078, 2 balls
- light green 9936, 1 ball
- bright yellow 9935, 1 ball
- black 0059, 2 balls
- orange 9934, 4 (4) 5 balls
- pink 9932, 1 ball
Needles: 4½ mm needles

Tension: 10 x 10 cm in garter stitch on 4½ mm needles equal 17 sts and 20 garters.
S/M: ☐ = 10 sts and 8 garters
L: ☐ = 12 sts and 8 garters
Knitting method: The sweater is knitted back and forth using garter stitch and intarsia technique.
Garter stitch: 1 garter = 2 rows k worked back and forth

Front: Cast on 70 (84) sts using 4½ mm needles and black yarn. Knit pattern A in garter st. N.B.: S/M: ☐ = 10 sts and 8 garters, L: ☐ = 12 sts and 8 garters. Increases and decreases are knitted as follows: between a and b decrease on both sides *1 st in each garter once (twice) and after 3 garters 1 more st, repeat five times from*. Between c and d, increase on both sides *1 st in each garter two (four) times and 1 st in each second (third) garter three times (once), repeat four times from*. Between d and e, increase on both sides *1 st in each garter once (twice) and after 3 garters 1 more st, repeat five times from*. Knit the collar by casting off 10 (12) sts in every eigth garter. Knit 2 more garters with black yarn. Cast off.
Back: Knit the back like the front except using pattern B.
Sleeves: Sew collar seams down to e. Pick up 60 (66) sts using 4½ mm needles and orange yarn: e indicates the center of the shoulder and d indicates the armpit. Knit in garter st. When the sleeve measures approx. 40 (41) cm knit 6 cm with acorn heather yarn and 2 garters with black yarn. Cast off.
Finishing: Sew side seams and underarm seams. Darn in loose ends.

5 Eight-petal rose sweater

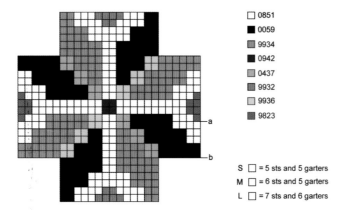

☐	0851
■	0059
▦	9934
■	0942
▥	0437
▦	9932
▨	9936
▦	9823

S ☐ = 5 sts and 5 garters
M ☐ = 6 sts and 5 garters
L ☐ = 7 sts and 6 garters

Inserts: Textile Museum, Halldóra's room, Blönduós.

Size: S (M) L
Width at hips: approx. 82 (98) 115 cm
Materials: Loðband - einband from Ístex
- white 0851, 3 balls
- black 0059, 2 balls
- orange 9934, 2 balls
- dark blue 0942, 1 ball
- light blue 0437, 1 ball
- pink 9932, 1 ball
- light green 9936, 1 ball
- green 9823, 1 ball
Needles: 4 mm and 4½ mm needles, 4 mm crochet hook
Tension: 10 x 10 cm in garter stitch on 4½ mm needles equal 17 sts and 20 garters.
S: ☐ = 5 sts and 5 garters
M: ☐ = 6 sts and 5 garters
L: ☐ = 7 sts and 6 garters

Knitting method: The sweater is knitted back and forth using garter stitch and intarsia technique.

Garter stitch: 1 garter = 2 rows k worked back and forth

Front: Cast on 70 (84) 98 sts using 4½ mm needles and white yarn. Knit pattern in garter st. N.B.: S: □ = 5 sts and 5 garters, M: □ = 6 sts and 5 garters, L: □ = 7 sts and 6 garters. Upon reaching the armhole, cast on 30 (36) 42 sts on each side for the sleeves. Upon reaching the shoulder cast off 30 (36) 42 sts on each side and knit the collar. When the pattern is complete, cast off with white yarn.

Back: Knit the back like the front.

Finishing: Sew side seams and sleeve seams. Pick up 30 (36) 42 sts at mid-sleeve on 4 mm needles with white yarn, knit 24 (24) 25 cm ribbing (k1, p1) and 1 row as follows: continue purling every p but knit 3 sts in every other k. Cast off. Sew underarm seams except between a and b. Darn in loose ends.

6 A second eight-petal rose sweater

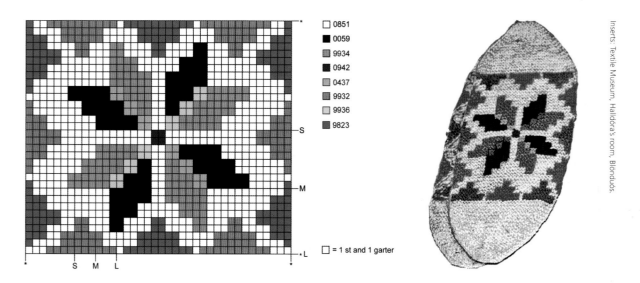

□	0851
■	0059
▨	9934
■	0942
▨	0437
▨	9932
▨	9936
▨	9823

□ = 1 st and 1 garter

Inserts: Textile Museum, Halldóra's room, Blönduós.

111

Size: S (M) L
Width: approx. 98 (103) 110 cm
Length to armhole: approx. 26 (30) 34 cm
Materials: Loðband - einband from Ístex
- white 0851, 3 (3) 4 balls
- black 0059, 2 balls
- orange 9934, 2 balls
- dark blue 0942, 1 ball
- light blue 0437, 1 ball
- pink 9932, 1 ball
- light green 9936, 1 ball
- green 9823, 1 ball
Needles: 4 mm and 4½ mm needles, 4 mm crochet hook
Tension: 10 x 10 cm using garter stitch and intarsia technique on 4½ mm needles equal 19 sts and 18 garters.
□ = 1 st and 1 garter
Knitting method: The sweater is knitted back and forth in one piece using garter stitch and intarsia technique.
Garter stitch: 1 garter = 2 rows k worked back and forth

Front: Start knitting the front. Cast on 90 (98) 104 sts using 4½ mm needles and white yarn. Knit pattern in garter st beginning at the appropriate mark according to size. N.B.: □ = 1 st and 1 garter. Repeat pattern from *-* to end of row and also from *-* upward. After 15 garters and 1 pattern (53 garters) 1 pattern and 28 garters, cast on 58 (62) 66 sts on each side for the sleeves. After 15 garters and 2 patterns (23 garters and 2 patterns) 3 patterns, mark the collar as follows: knit 64 (68) 72 sts, knit the next 78 (86) 92 sts with a contrasting color yarn, return them to left needle and continue knitting the pattern (using new bobbins) along with the last 64 (68) 72 sts.
Back: Now, continue knitting the back as a mirror image of the front. Cast off with white yarn.
Collar: Knit collar as follows: draw out contrasting color yarn and place the back sts on a stitch holder or length of yarn. Place the front sts on needles and continue knitting the pattern. After 2 patterns uppward cast off with white yarn. Set the saved back sts on needles and knit the same way as front sts.

Finishing: Pick up 63 (67) 71 sts from the sleeves using 4 mm needles and white yarn, knit 10 (11) 12 cm ribbing (k1, p1) and 1 row as follows: continue purling every p but knit 3 sts in every other k. Cast off. Sew side seams and underarm seams. Darn in loose ends.

7 Rose-pattern sweater

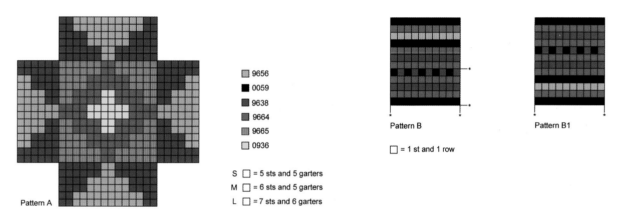

Pattern A

Pattern B

Pattern B1

9656
0059
9638
9664
9665
0936

☐ = 1 st and 1 row

S ☐ = 5 sts and 5 garters
M ☐ = 6 sts and 5 garters
L ☐ = 7 sts and 6 garters

Size: S (M) L
Width: approx. 74 (88) 103 cm
Length: approx. 46 (46) 54 cm
Materials: Kambgarn from Ístex
- **turquoise blue 9656, 2 (2) 3 balls**
- **green 9638, 2 (2) 3 balls**
- **red 9664, 1 ball**
- **black 0059, 1 ball**
- **orange 9665, 1 ball**
- **bright yellow 0936, 1 ball**

Inserts: National Museum of Iceland, Ethnological Collections (1) and Skógar District Museum (2).

Needles: 4 mm and 4½ mm needles, 3 mm crochet hook
Tension: 10 x 10 cm in garter stitch on 4½ mm needles equal 19 sts and 20 garters.
S: □ = 5 sts and 5 garters
M: □ = 6 sts and 5 garters
L: □ = 7 sts and 6 garters
Pattern B and B1: □ = 1 st and 1 row
Knitting method: The sweater is knitted back and forth in one piece using garter stitch and intarsia technique.
Garter stitch: 1 garter = 2 rows k worked back and forth

Sweater: Cast on 70 (84) 98 sts using 4 mm needles and black yarn. Knit pattern B in rib (k1, p1). N.B.: □ = 1 st and 1 row. Repeat pattern from *-* to end of row. Change to 4½ mm needles and knit pattern A in garter st. N.B.: S: □ = 5 sts and 5 garters, M: □ = 6 sts and 5 garters, L: □ = 7 sts and 6 garters. Upon reaching the armhole, cast on 40 (48) 52 sts on each side for the sleeves. At mid-pattern cast off 50 (52) 54 sts in the middle for the neck opening and cast them back on in the next row. Upon reaching armhole again, cast off 40 (48) 56 sts on both sides. When the pattern is complete, change to 4 mm needles and knit pattern B1 in rib (k1, p1). N.B.: □ = 1st and 1 row. Repeat pattern from *-* to end of row. Cast off with black yarn.

Finishing: Pick up 70 (70) 84 sts from the sleeves using 4 mm needles and black yarn and knit pattern B in rib (k1, p1) from *-* upward. N.B.: □ = 1 st and 1 row. Repeat pattern from *-* to end of row. Cast off alternating black and green yarn. Sew side seams and underarm seams. Crochet an edging around the neck opening using sc, 3 mm crochet hook and black yarn. Darn in loose ends.

Needles: 6 mm circular needle, 80 cm long; 4½ mm circular needle, 40 cm long and 6 mm double pointed needles

Tension: 10 x 10 cm in stocking stitch on 6 mm needles equal 13 sts and 18 rows.

□ = 1 st and 1 row

Knitting method: The body and sleeves are knitted in the round in stocking stitch. At the armhole, the sts of the sleeves and the body are combined on one needle and the yoke is knitted in the round using Fair Isle knitting technique. When knitting the pattern, be careful to keep a slack on the yarn in order to ensure an easy fit. An opening is cut for the zipper. The pattern is embroidered with Swiss darning.

Moss st: ** *k1, p1, repeat from*, in the next row *p1, k1 repeat from*, repeat from**.

Body: Cast on 112 (128) 136 (144) 160 sts using 6 mm circular needle and black sheep heather lopi yarn and knit back and forth 2 rows moss st. Join in a circle and cast on 2 extra sts which are purled (sts to cut for zipper opening). There are 114 (130) 138 (146) 162 sts on the needle. Knit in the round in stocking st until the body measures approx. 35 (36) 38 (40) 43 cm. Set body aside. Don't break off yarn.

Sleeves: Cast on 30 (32) 34 (36) 40 sts using 6 mm double-pointed needles and black sheep heather lopi yarn. Join in a circle and knit 2 rows moss st in the round then stocking st. Increase 2 sts (1 st after the first st and 1 st after the last st in the row) in every thirteenth (thirteenth) twelfth (eleventh) eleventh row five (six) seven (eight) eight times. There are then 40 (44) 48 (52) 56 sts on the needles. When the sleeve measures approx. 45 (49) 52 (52) 54 cm, set aside 8 (10) 10 (10) 12 sts from the underarm midpoint of sleeve on a stitch holder or length of yarn. Set sleeve aside. Knit the other sleeve in the same way.

Yoke: Combine the body and sleeves on 6 mm circular needle as follows: knit, using black sheep heather lopi yarn, the first 25 (28) 30 (32) 35 sts of the right front (extra purled st included), and place the next 8 (10) 10 (10) 12 sts of the body on a stitch holder or length of yarn. Continue knitting the 32 (34) 38 (42) 44 sts of the first sleeve. Then knit 48 (54) 58 (62) 68 sts of the back piece, and place the next 8 (10) 10 (10) 12 sts on a stitch holder or length of yarn. Knit the 32 (34) 38 (42) 44 sts of the second sleeve. Knit the 25 (28) 30 (32) 35 remaining sts of the left front (extra purled st included). There are now 162 (176) 194 (210) 226 sts on the needle. Knit pattern. Repeat it from *-* to end of row and decrease as shown on chart. Begin and end with the purled sts. When the pattern is complete, there are 72 (79) 86 (93) 100 sts left on the needle. Knit 1 row using black sheep heather lopi yarn and decrease 18 (25) 30 (37) 42 sts evenly spaced. Cast off extra purled sts. There are 54 (54) 56 (56) 58 sts on the needle. Change to 4½ mm circular needle and knit back and forth 4 cm ribbing (k1, p1). Cast off.

Finishing: Embroider the pattern using Swiss darning as shown on chart. Graft together the underarm sts. Machine-sew a double seam on each side of the purled sts at the center front using a small, straight stitch. Cut between the seams. Crochet a trim at the front edges using sc, 4 mm crochet hook and black sheep heather lopi yarn. Sew the zipper in by hand, then by machine. The seam is hidden by the edging. Fold the collar in half toward the inside and sew down loosely. Darn in loose ends.

13 Infant's cardigan and bonnet

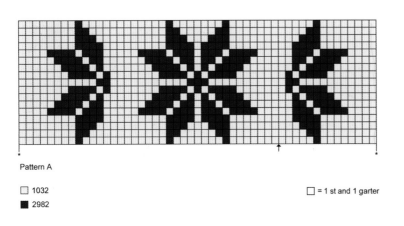

Pattern A

☐ 1032
■ 2982

☐ = 1 st and 1 garter

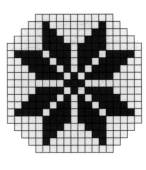

Pattern B

Size: 0-3 months
Width: approx. 49 cm
Length: approx. 24 cm
Sleeve length: approx. 12 cm
Materials: Kitten Mohair from SandnesGarn
- white 1001, 1 ball
- brown 2982, 1 ball
- gray 1032, 2 balls
Needles: 4 mm needles, 4 mm double pointed needles,
3 mm crochet hook

Two gray buttons

Tension: 10 x 10 cm in garter stitch on 4 mm needles equal 21 sts and 20 garters.

□ = 1 st and 1 garter

Knitting method: The cardigan is knitted back and forth in one piece, beginning from the back, using garter stitch and intarsia technique.

Garter stitch: 1 garter = 2 rows k worked back and forth.

Circular garter stitch: 1 garter = 1 row k, 1 row p

Picot edging: crochet 1 slip st and then *1 small picot (2 chain sts, 1 slip st in first chain st), pass over 1 st, 1 sc in next st, repeat from*.

Cardigan: Back: Cast on 51 sts using 4 mm needles and gray yarn. Knit in garter st. After 14 garters begin knitting pattern A from * til *. N.B.: □ = 1 st and 1 garter. After a total of 27 garters, cast on 25 sts on each side for the sleeves. After 20 garters from the armhole cast off 21 sts in the middle for the neck opening. Continue knitting each set of 40 sts individually as follows:

Left front (on the left): Knit 1 garter then increase on right side for the neck opening 1 st in each row ten times and in the next row cast on 13 sts. Continue knitting 5 garters, then pattern A from the arrow to *. After 42 garters from the armhole, cast off 25 sts for the sleeve. Knit 27 more garters and cast off.

Right front: Cast on 3 sts using 4 mm needles and gray yarn. Knit in garter st. Increase on right side 1 st in each row 10 times. Set the 13 sts aside. Knit the 40 sts as follows: knit 1 garter, then increase on left side for the neck opening 1 st in each row ten times. Place on needles (left side) the 13 sts that were set aside. Knit 5 garters, then knit 1 st and begin knitting pattern A from * to arrow. After 42 garters from the armhole, cast off 25 sts for the sleeve. Knit 27 more garters and cast off.

Finishing: Sew side seams and sleeve seams. Crochet a sc edging around the neck opening and wrist and a picot edging at the lower edge of cardigan, using 3 mm crochet hook and white yarn. Crochet buttonholes with chain st using 3 mm crochet hook and gray yarn on each side of the neckline. Sew the buttons on. Darn in loose ends.

Bonnet: Cast on 11 sts using 4 mm needles and gray yarn. Knit pattern B in garter st. N.B.: □ = 1 st and 1 garter. Sts are cast on or cast off in each garter in order to create an octagon as shown on chart. Cast off. Pick up 120 sts around the octagon using 4 mm double-pointed needles and gray yarn and knit 10 garters in circular garter st. Cast off 90 sts. Knit the 30 sts that are left back and forth in garter st and cast off on each side 1 st in each garter four times, then remaining sts.

Finishing: Using 3 mm crochet hook and white yarn, crochet a picot edging on the front edges of the bonnet and, using chain st, an approx. 17 cm long cord on each side of the face. Darn in loose ends.

14 Infant's set

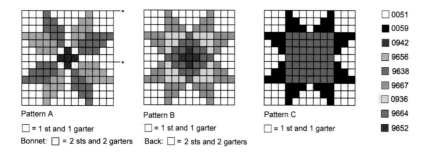

Pattern A

☐ = 1 st and 1 garter

Bonnet: ☐ = 2 sts and 2 garters

Pattern B

☐ = 1 st and 1 garter

Back: ☐ = 2 sts and 2 garters

Pattern C

☐ = 1 st and 1 garter

☐ 0051
■ 0059
■ 0942
☐ 9656
■ 9638
■ 9667
☐ 0936
■ 9664
■ 9652

Inserts: Textile Museum, Halldóra's room, Blönduós (1), National Museum of Iceland, Ethnological Collections (2) and Skógar District Museum (3).

Size: 0-3 (3-6) 6-9 months
Width: approx. 54 (57) 60 cm
Cardigan length: approx. 23 (26) 29 cm
Sleeve length: approx. 14 (17) 20 cm
Leg lenght: approx. 15 (18) 21 cm
Materials: Kambgarn from Ístex
- white 0051, 5 (5) 6 balls
- black 0059, 1 ball
- turquoise blue 9656, 1 ball
- dark blue 0942, 1 ball
- red 9664, 1 ball
- green 9638, 1 ball
- light green 9667, 1 ball
- bright yellow 0936, 1 ball
- brown 9652, 1 ball
Needles: 2½ mm and 3 mm needles, 2½ mm double-pointed needles, 3 mm crochet hook
Elastic band approx. 52 (60) 66 cm long
Tension: 10 x 10 cm in garter stitch on 3 mm needles equal 23 sts and 26 garters.
□ = 1 st and 1 garter
Back and bonnet front: □ = 2 sts and 2 garters
Knitting method: The set is knitted back and forth using garter stitch and intarsia technique.
Garter stitch: 1 garter = 2 rows k worked back and forth.
Picot edging: crochet 1 slip st and then *1 small picot (2 chain sts, 1 slip st in first chain st), pass over 1 st, 1 sc in next st, repeat from*.
Cord: *k3, push the sts over to the other end of the needle, repeat from*.

Cardigan: Right front: Cast on 31 (33) 35 sts using 3 mm needles and white yarn. Knit in garter st. When the front measures approx. 3 (5) 7 cm, knit 11 sts and begin knitting pattern A. N.B.: □ = 1 st and 1 garter. When the front measures approx. 12.5 (14.5) 16.5 cm, shape armhole by casting off 3 sts on the left side. Knit 2 more garters, then knit 5 sts and begin knitting pattern B. N.B.: □ = 1 st and 1 garter. After 17 (17) 19 garters from the armhole, cast off for the neck opening 8 sts on the right side, then 1 st in each garter twice and 1 st in the next garter. Knit 2 more garters and cast off.

Left front: Knit the left front as a mirror image of the right front except the roses which are knitted as follows: when the front measures approx. 9 (11) 13 cm, knit 16 (19) 22 sts and begin knitting pattern C. N.B.: □ = 1 st and 1 garter. When the front measures approx. 15 (17) 19 cm, knit 4 (7) 10 sts and begin knitting pattern A. N.B.: □ = 1 st and 1 garter.

Back: Cast on 62 (66) 70 sts using 3 mm needles and white yarn. Knit in garter st. When the back measures approx. 8 (10) 12 cm, begin knitting pattern B in the middle. N.B.: □ = 2 sts and 2 garters. When the back measures approx. 12.5 (14.5) 16.5 cm, shape armhole by casting off 3 sts on each side. Knit 24 (24) 26 more garters and cast off.

Right sleeve: Cast on 31 (31) 33 sts using 2½ mm needles and white yarn. Knit 8 rows ribbing (k1, p1). Change to 3 mm needles and knit in garter st. Increase 6 sts evenly spaced and then on each side 1 st in every fourth (fifth) fifth garter seven (seven) eight times. When the sleeve measures approx. 7.5 (9) 12 cm, knit pattern C in the middle. N.B.: □ = 1 st and 1 garter. When the sleeve measures approx. 15 (17) 20 cm, cast off.

Left sleeve: Knit the left sleeve like the right one but without the rose.

Finishing: Sew shoulder seams. Sew sleeves into armholes. Sew side seams and underarm seams. Crochet a picot edging at the edge of the right front and around the neck opening using a 3 mm crochet hook and white yarn, adding a crocheted cord to each side of the neck opening as follows: crochet 40 chain sts, turn, pass over 1 chain st, *1 sc in next chain st, repeat 38 times from*, 1 sc in the edge. Continue crocheting the picot at the edge of the left front and lower edge of cardigan. Join in a circle with a slip st. Break off yarn. Darn in loose ends.

Pants: Cast on 37 (41) 41 sts using 2½ mm needles and white yarn. Knit 8 rows ribbing (k1, p1). Change to 3 mm needles and knit in garter st. In the first row increase 23 (29) 35 sts evenly spaced. When the pant leg measures approx. 15 (18) 21 cm, increase 1 st in each garter 8 (10) 10 times on each side for the crotch. There are then 76 (90) 96 sts on the needles. Cast off 8 (10) 10 sts on each side and set aside the 60 (70) 76 sts in the middle. Knit the other pant leg the same way. Place both pant legs on the needles, i.e. 120 (140) 152 sts. Continue knitting 3 more cm. Knit the pants higher up on the bottom as follows: at the beginning of the row, *k4, turn, slip 1 st, k3, turn, k8, turn, slip 1st, k7, turn, k12, turn, slip 1 st, k11, turn, k16, turn, slip 1 st, k15, turn, continue knitting. At the beginnig of the next row, repeat from*. Continue knitting. When the pants measure approx. 17 (21) 25 cm from the crotch, knit 4 rows k, 1 row p (folding seam), 4 rows k and cast off.

Finishing: Sew pant leg seams, crotch and back of pants seams. Fold at folding seam toward wrong side and sew down. Draw the elastic band through the waist.

Bonnet: Cast on 3 sts using 2½ mm double-pointed needles and white yarn and knit an approx. 25 cm cord, then change to 3 mm needles and knit in garter st. Increase on each side for the ear flap 1 st in each garter six times. Simultaneously, when 9 sts are on the needles begin knitting pattern B in the middle. N.B.: □ = 1 st and 1 garter. When there are 15 sts left, set aside. Knit the other ear flap in the same way except knit pattern C instead of pattern B. Set aside. Cast on 6 (8) 10 sts using 3 mm needles and white yarn, knit the 15 sts from the first ear flap, cast on 26 (34) 42 sts, knit the 15 sts from the second ear flap, cast on 6 (8) 10 sts. There are now 68 (80) 92 sts on the needles. Continue knitting. After 3 garters begin knitting pattern A from *-* upward in the middle front of the bonnet. N.B.: □ = 2 sts and 2 garters. When the bonnet measures approx.12 (13) 14 cm, k2 together in each garter until there are 9 (10) 11 sts left. Break off yarn and draw through the sts.

Finishing: Sew the bonnet seam. Crochet a picot edging using 3 mm crochet hook and white yarn along the front edge. Attach 3 pompons at the top. Darn in loose ends.

15 Child's blanket

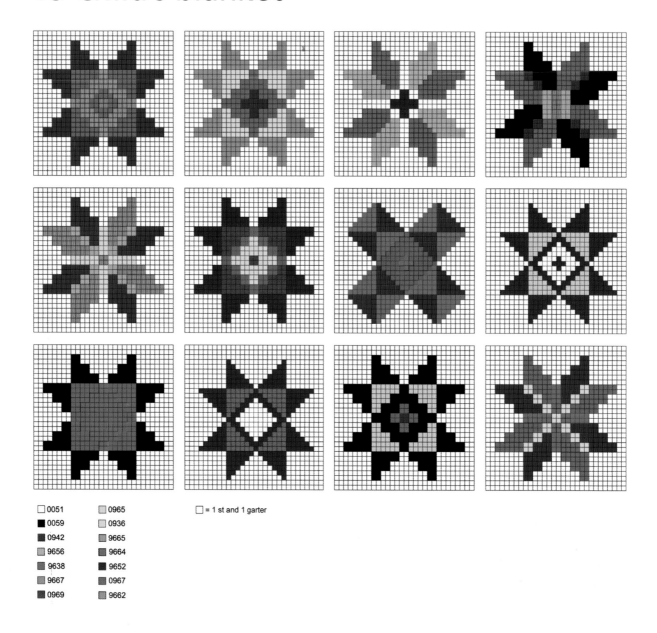

☐ 0051	☐ 0965	☐ = 1 st and 1 garter
■ 0059	☐ 0936	
■ 0942	■ 9665	
☐ 9656	■ 9664	
☐ 9638	■ 9652	
☐ 9667	■ 0967	
■ 0969	☐ 9662	

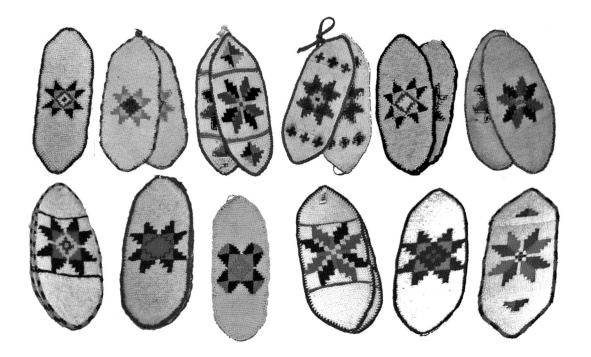

Inserts: Icelandic Handcrafts Society (1), National Museum of Iceland, Ethnological Collections (2 to 6), Skógar District Museum (7 to 9) and Textile Museum, Halldóra's room, Blönduós (10 to 12).

Size: approx. 68 x 98 cm
Materials: Kambgarn from Ístex
- **white 0051, 5 balls**
- **black 0059, 1 ball**
- **turquoise blue 9656, 1 ball**
- **dark blue 0942, 1 ball**
- **red 9664, 1 ball**
- **green 9638, 1 ball**
- **light green 9667, 1 ball**
- **dark green 0969, 1 ball**
- **bright yellow 0936, 1 ball**
- **orange 9665, 1 ball**

- brown 9652, 1 ball
- beige 0965, 1 ball
- hot pink 9662, 1 ball
Needles: 3 mm needles, 3 mm crochet hook
Tension: 10 x 10 cm using garter stitch and intarsia technique on 3 mm needles equal 23 sts and 26 garters.
□ = 1 st and 1 garter
Knitting method: The squares are knitted back and forth using garter stitch and intarsia technique, then crocheted together. An edging is crocheted around the blanket.
Garter stitch: 1 garter = 2 rows k worked back and forth

Squares: Begin by knitting two times 12 squares with different patterns (24 squares altogether) as follows: cast on 30 sts using 3 mm needles and white yarn, knit 30 garters with the appropriate pattern, cast off and darn in loose ends. N.B.: □ = 1 st and 1 garter. Arrange the squares according to the picture and join them together by crocheting picot edging around a square as follows: attach yarn at a corner using a slip st. Crochet **1 picot (3 chain sts, 1 slip st in second chain st, 1 slip st in first chain st), 1 sc, *1 picot, pass over 1 st, 2 sc, repeat eight times from*, repeat three times from**, break off. There is 1 picot at each corner and there are 9 picots on each side. Crochet all the squares like this but join them together at the same time, through the picots, as follows: crochet 2 chain sts, slip the hook into the tip of the picot to be joined, pull the yarn through the sts, 1 slip st in second chain st, 1 slip st in first chain st. Crochet edging around the entire blanket as follows:
Edging: 1st round: Crochet 1 slip st in the corner picot (upper left on picture), ***crochet 4 chain sts, 1 dc in same corner picot, ** *4 chain sts, 1 sc in the next picot, repeat nine times from*, 4 chain sts, 1 dc in the picots that are linked together, repeat four times from**, 4 chain sts, 1 dc in same picot (corner picot),** *4 chain sts, 1 sc in the next picot, repeat nine times from*, 4 chain sts, 1 dc in the picots that are linked together, repeat six times from*, repeat twice from***, finish the round with 1 slip st. There is a total of 204 arches.
2nd round: Crochet 5 sc in each arch (204 arches).
3rd round: Crochet chain st arch over 2 arches and, in the corner, 1 chain st arch above the corner arch as follows: **crochet *8 chain sts, pass over 9 sts, 1 sc in next st, repeat 20 times

from*, at the corner crochet 8 chain sts, pass over 4 sts, 1 sc in next st, *8 chain sts, pass over 9 sts, 1 sc in the next st, repeat 30 times from*, at the corner crochet 8 chain sts, pass over 4 sts, 1 sc in next st, repeat twice from**.

4th round: Crochet *7 sc in the arch, 5 chain sts, slip the stich off the hook, poke the hook in the fourth sc counting backward. Draw the st that was slipped through to create a small arch. Crochet 3 sc, 1 small picot (2 chain sts, 1 sc in first chain st) and 3 sc in small arch. Crochet 3 more sc in the large arch and 1 picot (3 chain sts, 1 slip st in second chain st, 1 slip st in first chain st), repeat 104 times from*, finish the round with 1 slip st, break off. Darn in loose ends.

16 Child's sweater and bonnet

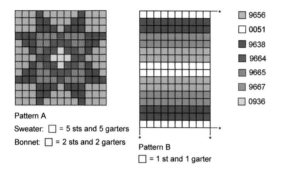

Pattern A
Sweater: ☐ = 5 sts and 5 garters
Bonnet: ☐ = 2 sts and 2 garters

Pattern B
☐ = 1 st and 1 garter

☐	9656
☐	0051
☐	9638
☐	9664
☐	9665
☐	9667
☐	0936

Inserts: National Museum of Iceland, Ethnological Collections (1) and Helga Þórarinsdóttir (2).

Size: 6 months (1 year) 2 years
Width: approx. 68 (72) 76 cm
Length: approx. 30 (34) 38 cm
Sleeve length: approx. 17 (20) 24 cm
Materials: Kambgarn from Ístex
- white 0051, 1 ball
- turquoise blue 9656, 2 (2) 3 balls
- green 9638, 1 ball
- light green 9667, 1 ball
- red 9664, 1 ball
- orange 9665, 1 ball
- bright yellow 0936, 1 ball
Needles: 3½ mm needles, 3½ mm double-pointed needles, 3 mm crochet hook
Tension: 10 x 10 cm using garter stitch and intarsia technique on 3½ mm needles equal 20 sts and 24 garters.
Sweater: ☐ = 5 sts and 5 garters
Bonnet: ☐ = 2 sts and 2 garters

Knitting method: The set is knitted back and forth using garter stitch and intarsia technique.
Garter stitch: 1 garter = 2 rows k worked back and forth
Circular garter stitch: 1 garter = 1 row k, 1 row p

Sweater: Front: Cast on 69 (73) 77 sts using 3½ mm needles and blue yarn. Knit in garter st. After 5 (7) 9 garters, knit pattern A in the middle. N.B.: □ = 5 sts and 5 garters. After a total of 65 (69) 73 garters, cast off for the neck opening 15 (17) 19 sts in the middle and on each side 2 sts, then 1 st in each garter three times. Knit each shoulder individually. Cast off after 5 (7) 9 garters from the pattern.

Back: Knit the back like the front but don't start casting off for the neck opening until there are 2 (4) 6 garters from the pattern, then cast off 19 (21) 23 sts in the middle, and on each side 2 sts then 1 st in each garter. Cast off remaining sts.

Sleeves: Cast on 50 (52) 54 sts using 3½ mm needles and blue yarn. Knit in garter st. Increase 1 st on each side in every fourth (fourth) fifth garter ten times. When the sleeve measures approx. 17 (20) 24 cm, cast off.

Finishing: Sew shoulder seams. Sew sleeves into armholes. Sew side seams and sleeve seams. Pick up 66 (70) 74 sts around the neck opening using 3½ mm double-pointed needles and blue yarn and knit 2 garters in circular garter st. Cast off loosely. Darn in loose ends.

Bonnet: *Cast on 30 (34) 38 sts using 3½ mm needles and blue yarn. Knit in garter st. After 2 (4) 6 garters, knit pattern A in the middle. N.B.: □ = 2 sts and 2 garters. When the pattern is complete, knit 2 (4) 6 more garters with blue yarn, then cast off. Repeat from*. Cast on 59 (67) 75 sts using 3½ mm needles and white yarn and knit pattern B in garter st. N.B.: □ = 1 st and 1 garter. Repeat pattern from *-* to end of row. Cast off.

Finishing: Sew bonnet seams. Take care that the garters lie correctly. Pick up 76 (84) 92 sts around the face using 3½ mm needles and blue yarn and knit 2 garters. Cast off. Crochet an edging at the nape of the neck using 3 mm crochet hook and blue yarn as follows:
1st row: Crochet sc in the edge.
2nd row: Crochet sc in the first 11 (13) 15 sts then in every other st until 11 (13) 15 sts are left. Crochet sc into these 11 (13) 15 sts.
3rd row: Crochet sc in each st.
4th row: Worked like 2nd row. Add a cord on each side of the face as follows: crochet 45 chain sts using 3 mm crochet hook and doubled blue yarn and attach the cord to the edge with 1 slip st. Darn in loose ends.

17 Blue child's sweater with roses

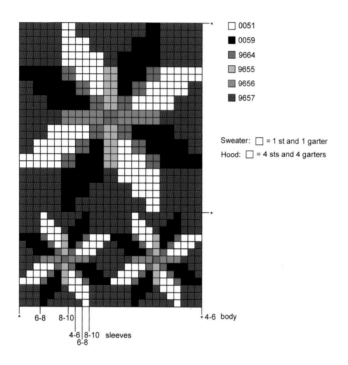

- 0051
- 0059
- 9664
- 9655
- 9656
- 9657

Sweater: ☐ = 1 st and 1 garter
Hood: ☐ = 4 sts and 4 garters

6-8   8-10   4-6 body

4-6 8-10   sleeves
6-8

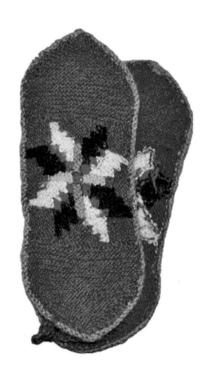

Size: 4-6 (6-8) 8-10 years
Width: approx. 74 (80) 88 cm
Length: approx. 36 (41) 46 cm
Sleeve length: approx. 30 (34) 38 cm
Materials: Kambgarn from Ístex
- white 0051, 2 (2) 3 balls
- black 0059, 2 (2) 3 balls
- red 9664, 1 ball

- light blue 9655, 1 ball
- turquoise blue 9656, 1 ball
- bright blue 9657, 6 (7) 8 balls

Needles: 3½ mm needles, 3 mm crochet hook

Tension: 10 x 10 cm using garter stitch and intarsia technique on 3½ mm needles equal 21 sts and 22 garters.

Sweater: □ = 1 st and 1 garter

Hood: □ = 4 sts and 4 garters

Knitting method: The sweater is knitted back and forth using garter stitch and intarsia technique.

Garter stitch: 1 garter = 2 rows k worked back and forth

Front: Cast on 78 (84) 92 using 3½ mm needles and bright blue yarn. Knit in garter st. Knit pattern beginning at the appropriate mark according to size. N.B.: □ = 1 st and 1 garter. Repeat pattern from *-* to end of row and also from *-* upward. When the front measures approx. 22 (23) 24 cm, cast off 3 sts for the armhole on each side. When the piece measures approx. 34 (36) 38 sts, cast off for the neck opening 14 (16) 18 sts in the middle, then on each side 2 sts in every garter 3 times and 1 st in every garter 3 times. Knit each shoulder individually. When the front measures approx. 38 (40) 42 cm, shape shoulder by casting off 7 (8) 9 sts in each garter twice, then remaining sts.

Back: Knit the back like the front but don't start casting off for the neck opening until it measures approx. 36 (38) 40 cm, then cast off 24 (26) 28 sts in the middle and on each side 1 st in every garter 4 times. When the back measures approx. 38 (40) 42 cm, shape shoulder as on front.

Sleeves: Cast on 42 (44) 46 sts using 3½ mm needles and bright blue yarn. Knit in garter st. Knit pattern beginning at the appropriate mark according to size. Repeat pattern from *-* to end of row and also from *-* upward. Increase 1 st on each side in every fifth (fifth) sixth garter 13 times. There are 66 (70) 74 sts on the needles. When the sleeve measures approx. 30 (34) 38 cm, cast off.

Finishing: Sew shoulder seams. Sew sleeves into armholes. Sew side seams and underarm seams.

Hood: Pick up 70 (74) 78 sts around the neck opening using 3½ mm needles and bright blue yarn. Begin in the middle of the front. After 5 (7) 9 garters, increase 26 sts evenly spaced and knit pattern in the middle from *-* upward. N.B.: ☐ = 4 sts and 4 garters. When the hood measures approx. 30 (32) 34 cm, cast off.

Finishing: Graft the top of the hood together. Crochet an edging in every other garter around the hood using sc, 3 mm crochet hook and blue yarn. Darn in loose ends.

18 Sylvia's pink sweater and cap

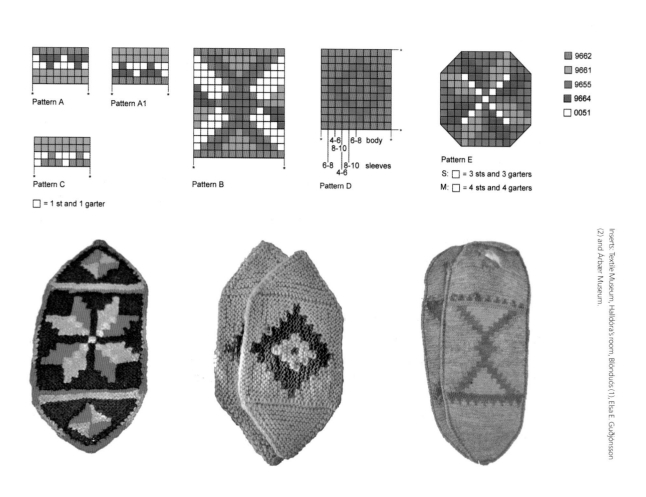

Pattern A

Pattern A1

Pattern C

Pattern B

4-6 | 6-8 body
8-10
6-8 | 8-10 sleeves
4-6

Pattern D

9662
9661
9655
9664
0051

Pattern E

S: ☐ = 3 sts and 3 garters
M: ☐ = 4 sts and 4 garters

☐ = 1 st and 1 garter

Inserts: Textile Museum, Halldóra's room, Blönduós (1), Elsa E. Guðjónsson (2) and Árbær Museum.

Size: 2-4 (4-6) 6-8 years
Width: approx. 63 (71) 81 cm
Length: approx. 38 (43) 48 cm
Sleeve length: approx. 30 (34) 38 cm
Cap size: S (M)
Materials: Kambgarn from Ístex
- hot pink 9662, 4 (4) 5 balls
- pink 9661, 1 ball
- light blue 9655, 2 (2) 3 balls
- red 9664, 1 ball
- white 0051, 1 ball
Needles: 3½ mm needles, 3½ mm double pointed needles, 3½ mm circular needle, 60 cm long, 3 mm crochet hook
Pink zipper
Tension: 10 x 10 cm using stocking stitch and Fair Isle technique on 3½ mm needles equal 29 sts and 30 garters.
□ = 1 st and 1 garter
Knitting method: The border at the lower edge of sweater and sleeves i knitted back and forth using garter stitch and intarsia technique. The sts are then placed on a circular needle and knit in a circle using Fair Isle technique and stocking stitch. An opening is cut for the sleeves, neckline and zipper.
Garter stitch: 1 garter = 2 rows k worked back and forth
Circular garter stitch: 1 garter = 1 row k, 1 row p

Body: Cast on 182 (208) 234 sts using 3½ mm needles and pink yarn. Knit pattern A, then B and C back and forth in garter st. N.B.: □ = 1 st and 1 garter. Repeat pattern from *-* to end of row. Join in circle on 3½ mm circular needle and cast on 4 extra sts that are purled (sts to cut for zipper opening). Knit pattern D in the round beginning at the appropriate mark according to size using Fair Isle technique and stocking st. Increase 1 st in the first row. Repeat pattern from *-* to end of row and also from *-* upward. When the body measures approx. 38 (43) 48 cm, cast off.

Sleeves: Cast on 55 (61) 67 sts using 3½ mm double-pointed needles and pink yarn. Knit pattern A back and forth in garter st. Repeat pattern from *-* to end of row. Join in a circle and knit 2 garters with pink yarn and circular garter st. Knit pattern D beginning at the appropriate mark according to size using Fair Isle technique and stocking st. Repeat pattern from *-* to end of row and also from *-* upward. Increase1 st on each side in every sixth (sixth) seventh garter 12 times. There are 79 (85) 91 sts. When the sleeve measures approx. 30 (34) 38 cm, cast off.

Finishing: Sew border seams at the cuffs. Mark the armhole opening from the shoulder down. Machine-sew a double seam on each side of the marking using a fine, straight stitch. Machine-sew a double seam on both sides of the purled sts in the middle of the front using a fine, straight stitch. Cut between the seams. Graft or sew shoulder seams. Sew sleeves into armholes. Mark the neck opening: 12 (13) 14 cm wide, 1 cm down at the center back and 4 cm down at the center front. Between these marks, mark the curve of the neckline. Machine-sew a double seam using a fine, straight stitch along the marking. Cut away excess material. Pick up 68 (74) 80 sts around the neck opening using 3½ mm needles and red yarn and knit 2 garters. Cast off loosely. Crochet an edging at the front edges using sc, 3 mm crochet hook and pink yarn. Sew the zipper in place by hand and then by machine. The seam is hidden by the edging. Darn in loose ends.

Cap: Cast on 21 (28) sts using 3½ mm needles and blue yarn. Knit pattern E back and forth in garter st. N.B.: S: □ = 3 sts and 3 garters, M: □ = 4 sts and 4 garters. Sts are cast on or cast off in each garter in order to create an octagon as shown on chart. Cast off. Pick up 120 (140) sts around the octagon and knit 2 garters in the round using 3½ mm double-pointed needles and pink yarn. Knit 1 row with hot pink yarn then pattern D. Repeat pattern from *-* to end of row. Knit 1 row with hot pink yarn then pattern A1. Repeat pattern from *-* to end of row. Cast off.

Finishing: Darn in loose ends.

19 Flowerpot sweater with hood

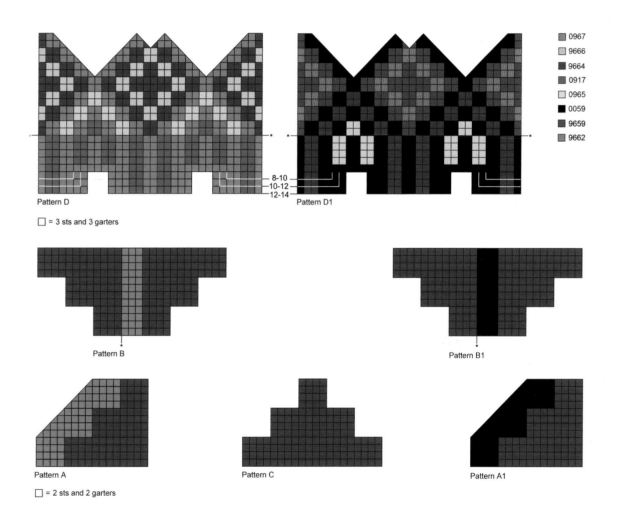

	0967
	9666
	9664
	0917
	0965
	0059
	9659
	9662

Pattern D

□ = 3 sts and 3 garters

8-10
10-12
12-14

Pattern D1

Pattern B

Pattern B1

Pattern A

□ = 2 sts and 2 garters

Pattern C

Pattern A1

Size: 8-10 (10-12) 12-14 years
Width: approx. 90 (96) 102 cm
Length: approx. 52 (56) 60 cm
Sleeve length: approx. 38 (41) 44 cm
Materials: Kambgarn from Ístex
Gray sweater:
- gray 0967, 7 (8) 9 balls
- yellow 9666, 1 ball
- red 9664, 1 ball
- bright red 0917, 1 ball
- beige 0965, 1 ball
Black sweater:
- black 0059, 6 (6) 7 balls
- hot pink 9662, 1 ball
- red 9664, 2 balls
- beige 0965, 1 ball
- violet 9659, 1 ball
Needles: 4 and 4½ mm needles, 3 mm crochet hook
Gray/black zipper
Tension: 10 x 10 cm using garter stitch and intarsia technique on 4½ mm needles equal 19 sts and 20 garters.
Sweater: □ = 2 st and 2 garters
Hood: □ = 3 sts and 3 garters
Knitting method: The sweater and the hood are knitted back and forth using garter stitch and intarsia technique.
Garter stitch: 1 garter = 2 rows k worked back and forth

Right front: Cast on 42 (46) 48 sts using 4½ mm needles and gray/black yarn. Knit 12 garters. Knit pocket as follows: place the first 3 sts and the last 7 (11) 13 sts in the row on a stitch holder or length of yarn. Change to 4 mm needles and knit the 32 sts in the middle with pattern A/A1 and doubled yarn. N.B.: □ = 2 sts and 2 garters. After 8 garters, cast off 1 st in each garter sixteen times as shown on chart (slip first st to make the edge prettier). When the pocket is complete, place the 16 remaining sts on a stitch holder or length of yarn. Change to 4½ mm needles and knit the 3 gray/black sts that were set aside, pick up 32 sts from the wrong side at the bottom of the pocket and knit the 7 (11) 13 sts that were set aside. Knit 24 garters. Fasten the pocket to the sweater as follows: knit 3 sts, then the next 16 sts together with the 16 sts that were set aside. Continue knitting. When the front measures approx. 31 (34) 36 cm, cast off 3 sts on the left side for the armhole. When the front measures approx. 40 (44) 48 cm, knit pattern B/B1 at the beginning of the row from *-*. After 16 garters of pattern, cast off for the neck opening 9 (10) 11 sts on the right side, then 2 sts in each garter three times and 1 st in every garter twice. After 22 garters of pattern, shape shoulder by casting off 7 (8) 8 sts in each garter twice, then remaining sts.

Left front: Knit the left front as a mirror image of the right front.

Back: Cast on 84 (92) 96 sts using 4½ mm needles and gray/black yarn. Knit 12 garters, then pattern C in the middle. N.B.: □ = 2 sts and 2 garters. When the back measures approx. 31 (34) 36 cm, cast off 3 sts on each side for the armholes. When the back measures approx. 40 (44) 48 cm, knit pattern B/B1 in the middle. After 20 garters of pattern, cast off for the neck opening 22 (24) 26 in the middle, then on each side 2 sts in every garter three times. Knit each shoulder individually. After 22 garters of pattern, shape shoulder as on front.

Sleeves: Cast on 49 (53) 57 sts using 4 mm and gray/black yarn. Knit 5 cm ribbing (k1, p1). Change to 4½ mm needles and knit in garter st. In the first row increase 9 sts evenly spaced and then on each side 1 st in every fifth (sixth) seventh garter 12 (12) 13 times. There are 82 (86) 92 sts on the needles. When the sleeve measures approx. 43 (46) 51 cm, cast off.

Finishing: Sew shoulder seams. Sew sleeves into armholes. Sew side seams and underarm seams. Darn in loose ends.

Hood: Pick up 66 (72) 78 sts around the neck opening using 4½ mm needles as follows: 3 sts with gray/black yarn, 6 sts with bright red/red yarn, 15 (18) 21 sts with gray/black yarn, 6 sts with bright red yarn, 6 sts with gray/black yarn in the middle of the back, 6 sts with bright red/red yarn, 15 (18) 21 sts with gray/black yarn, 6 sts with bright red/red yarn and 3 sts with gray/black yarn. Knit pattern D/D1 in garter st. Begin knitting pattern upwards at the appropriate mark according to size. N.B.: □ = 3 sts and 3 garters. After 3 (6) 9 garters increase 15 (12) 9 sts evenly spaced on the 15 (18) 21 gray/black sts on each side as shown on chart. There are

96 sts on the needles. The decreases on the hood are knitted as follows: k2 together in every garter as shown on chart.

Finishing: Sew the top of the hood together. Sew pocket seams. Crochet an edging into the edge of the front opening and around the hood opening using sc, 3 mm crochet hook and gray/black yarn. N.B.: crochet into every other garter between *-* around the hood opening. Sew the zipper in place by hand and then by machine. The seam is hidden by the edging. Darn in loose ends.

20 Delicate mittens

Size: S (M) L
Materials: Loðband - einband from Ístex
Striped mittens:
- black sheep heather 0151, 2 balls
- acorn heather 0853, 1 ball
- oatmeal 0885, 1 ball
- light green 9936, 1 ball
Checkered mittens:
- white 0851, 2 balls
- acorn heather 0853, 1 ball
- light gray 1027, 1 ball
Needles: 2½ mm needles, 2 mm crochet hook
Tension: 10 x 10 cm in garter stitch on 2½ mm
needles equal 26 sts and 28 garters.
Knitting method: The mittens are closely knitted, back and forth using garter stitch and intarsia technique. Begin with the middle section, then the tips (wrist and fingers) and finally, the thumb.
Garter stitch: 1 garter = 2 rows k worked back and forth.

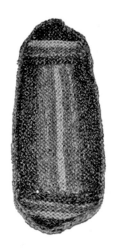

Middle section: cast on 34 (40) 46 sts using 2½ mm needles. Knit back of hand 24 (28) 32 garters in garter st. Knit 24 (28) 32 more garters for the palm but after 16 (18) 20 garters, divide the sts in half for thumb and continue knitting each set of 17 (20) 23 sts separately. Cast off after knitting the 8 (10) 12 remaining garters.

Tips: Pick up 48 (56) 64 sts from the selvedge of the middle section using 2½ mm needles. After knitting 6 garters, divide the sts in half and continue knitting each set of 24 (28) 32 sts separately. Cast off 1 st from each side in each garter 10 (12) 14 times. When 2 sts are left on the needles, break off yarn and draw through the sts. Knit the other tips the same way, picking up from the other selvedge.

Thumb: Pick up 16 (20) 24 sts from the edges using 2½ mm needles. After knitting 12 (14) 16 garters, divide the sts in half and continue knitting each set of 8 (10) 12 sts separately. Cast off on each side 1 st in each garter 3 (4) 5 times. When 2 sts are left on the needles, break off yarn and draw through the sts.

Finishing: Sew side seams and thumb. Take care in sewing the tips so that you have one left-hand and one right-hand mitten. Crochet an edging around the wrist using sc and 2 mm crochet hook. Close the round with 1 slip st and crochet a cord as follows: crochet 30 chain sts, turn, pass over 29th chain st *1 slip st in next chain. Repeat from* back to the mitten. Break yarn. Darn in loose ends.

Striped mittens: Main colour is black sheep heather. The stripes of the middle section are knitted in the middle of back of hand and of palm. They consist of 2 garters acorn heather yarn, 1 garter oatmeal yarn, 2 garters acorn heather yarn, 2 garters light green yarn, 2 garters acorn heather yarn, 1 garter oatmeal yarn, 2 garters acorn heather yarn. The stripes for the tips are knitted immediately after picking up from the middle section and consist of 1 garter oatmeal yarn, 2 garters acorn heather yarn and 2 garters light green yarn. The thumb is knitted using intarsia technique and consists of 6 (8) 10 sts black sheep heather yarn, 4 sts acorn heather yarn and 6 (8) 10 sts black sheep heather yarn. The edging and cord are crocheted with black sheep heather yarn.

Checkered mittens: Each check of the middle section consists of 17 (20) 23 sts acorn heather yarn, 17 (20) 23 sts white yarn and 12 (14) 16 garters. The checks of the tips consist of 12 (14) 16 sts acorn heather yarn, 12 (14) 16 sts white yarn and 10 garters. The thumb consists of 8 (10) 12 sts acorn heather yarn and 8 (10) 12 sts white yarn. The edging and cord are crocheted with light gray yarn.

21 Rose-pattern mittens and matching beret

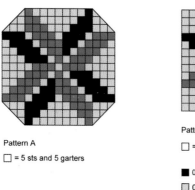

Pattern A

☐ = 5 sts and 5 garters

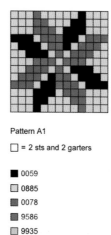

Pattern A1

☐ = 2 sts and 2 garters

■ 0059
☐ 0885
■ 0078
■ 9586
☐ 9935

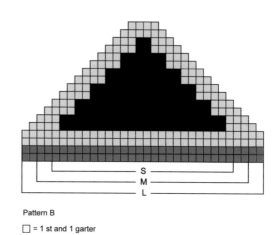

Pattern B

☐ = 1 st and 1 garter

Mittens: S (M) L
Beret: one size
Materials: Loðband - einband from Ístex
- white 00851, 1 ball
- bright red 0078, 1 ball
- bright yellow 9935, 1 ball
- green 9823, 1 ball
- oatmeal 0885, 3 balls
- black 0059, 2 balls
Needles: 2½ mm needles, 2½ mm circular needle, 2 mm crochet hook

Tension: 10 x 10 cm in garter stitch on 2½ mm needles equal 26 sts and 28 garters.

Beret: Pattern A: □ = 5 sts and 5 garters

Mittens: Pattern A1: □ = 2 sts and 2 garters **Pattern B:** □ = 1 st and 1 garter

Knitting method: The beret and the mittens are knitted back and forth using garter stitch and intarsia technique.

Garter stitch: 1 garter = 2 rows k worked back and forth

Circular garter stitch: 1 garter = 1 row k , 1 row p

Beret: Cast on 45 sts using 2½ mm needles and oatmeal yarn. Knit pattern A in garter st. N.B.: □ = 5 sts and 5 garters. Sts are cast on or cast off in each garter in order to create an octagon as shown on chart. Cast off. Pick up 220 sts from the wrong side around the octagon using 2½ mm circular needle and oatmeal yarn (35 sts from the straight edges and 20 sts from the diagonal edges). Knit in circular garter st. When the border measures approx. 5 cm, cast off 44 sts evenly spaced as follows: *k2 together, k3, repeat from* to end of row. There are 176 sts left on the needle. Knit 1 garter and cast off 44 sts evenly spaced as follows: *k2 together, k2, repeat from* to end of row. There are 132 sts left on the needle. Knit ribbing (k1, p1): 2 rows red yarn, 2 rows bright red yarn, 4 rows black yarn, 2 rows oatmeal yarn and 2 rows bright red yarn. Cast off.

Finishing: Crochet a trim around the beret using sc, 2 mm crochet hook and white yarn. Darn in loose ends.

Mittens: Knit the mittens as described on pages 146 and 147 with oatmeal yarn as main color. Knit pattern A1 in the center of the middle section back of hand beginning after 0 (1) 3 garters. N.B.: □ = 2 sts and 2 garters, knit pattern B on all four tips beginning immediately at the picked-up sts. Start at the appropriate mark for each size. N.B.: □ = 1 st and 1 garter. The edging and cord are crocheted with white yarn.

22 Cap, beret, bag and mittens

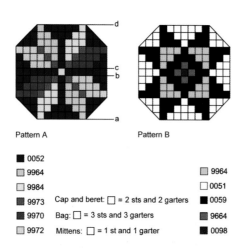

Pattern A   Pattern B

■ 0052
□ 9964
□ 9984
■ 9973   Cap and beret: □ = 2 sts and 2 garters
■ 9970   Bag: □ = 3 sts and 3 garters
□ 9972   Mittens: □ = 1 st and 1 garter

□ 9964
□ 0051
■ 0059
■ 9664
■ 0098

Inserts: Skógar District Museum (1) and Textile Museum, Halldóra's room, Blönduós (2).

Mittens size: S (M) L
Cap and beret: one size
Materials: Álafoss lopi from Ístex
Black sheep heather set:
- black sheep heather 0052, 4 balls
- raspberry heather 9970, 1 ball
- fairy green 9984, 1 ball
- golden heather 9964, 1 ball
- ecru heather 9972, 1 ball
- wheat heather 9973, 1 ball

White mittens and beret:
- white 0051, 3 balls
- black 0059, 1 ball
- happy red 0047, 1 ball
- sapphire blue heather 9968, 1 ball
- golden heather 9964, 1 ball

Needles: 5 mm double pointed needles, 5 mm circular needle, 60 cm. long, 6 and 7 mm needles, 5 mm crochet hook
Plastic tubing approx. 20 cm long and 1 cm in diameter, brown velcro approx. 3 cm long, lining material approx. 36 cm x 40 cm
Tension: 10 x 10 cm in garter stitch using 5 mm needles equal 12 sts and 14 garters.

Mittens: ☐ = 1 st and 1 garter
Cap and beret: ☐ = 2 sts and 2 garters
Bag: ☐ = 3 sts and 3 garters
Knitting method: The mittens are knitted in one piece, back and forth using garter stitch and intarsia technique, then the thumb. The cap and the beret are knitted back and forth using garter stitch and intarsia technique, then circular garter stitch.
Garter stitch: 1 garter = 2 rows k worked back and forth
Circular garter stitch: 1 garter = 1 row k and 1 row p

Right-hand mitten: Begin by knitting the wrist tips. Cast on 3 sts using 5 mm needles and main color yarn and knit in garter st. Increase 1 st in each garter on both sides five (six) seven times, set tip aside. Knit the other tip in the same way. Place both tips on needles and knit the middle section. After knitting 12 (13) 14 garters, mark the thumb as follows: at the beginning of the row, k1 then knit the next 6 (6) 7 sts with a contrasting color yarn, return them to left needle and continue knitting with main color. After 12 (13) 14 more garters, knit the finger tips by dividing the sts on two needles and making decreases on the mitten as follows: k2 together the first 2 sts and the last 2 sts on each needle in every garter until there are 6 sts left. Break off yarn and draw through the sts.

Thumb: Draw out contrasting color yarn and place sts on three needles. Pick up an extra st on each side in order to prevent gaps. Even out the sts so that half are on one needle and the other half is divided between the other two needles. In the first row, k2 together on each side (extra sts). After knitting 7 (8) 9 garters, begin decrease as follows: k2 together the first and last 2 sts on the first needle, the first 2 sts on the second needle and the last 2 sts on the third needle in each garter until there are 6 (6) 4 sts left. Break off yarn and draw through the sts.

Finishing: Sew side seams. Crochet an edging around the wrist using sc, 5 mm crochet hook. Finish the circle with 1 slip st and continue crocheting a cord of 20 chain sts. Break off yarn. Darn in loose ends.

Left-hand mitten: Knit in the same way as the right mitten except that the thumb is knitted on the other side as follows: at the end of the row, with 7 (7) 8 sts left, knit the next 6 (6) 7 sts with a contrasting color yarn, return them to left needle and continue knitting with main color.

Black sheep heather mittens: Pattern A is knitted in the middle of the back of the hand. N.B.: □ = 1 st and 1 garter. After 2 (3) 4 garters of the wrist tip, knit half a pattern, a to c on chart; after 2 (3) 4 garters from half pattern knit a whole pattern in the middle section of the mitten, a to d on chart; after 2 (3) 4 garters from the whole pattern, knit half a pattern on the finger tip, b to d on chart. The edging and cord are crocheted with black sheep heather.

White mittens: Pattern B is knitted in the middle of the back of the hand beginning after 6 (7) 8 garters of the middle section. The edging and cord are crocheted with black yarn.

Cap: Cast on 14 sts using 6 mm needles and black sheep heather yarn. Knit pattern A in garter st. N.B.: □ = 2 sts and 2 garters. Sts are cast on or cast off in each garter in order to create an octagon as shown on chart. When complete, cast off. Pick up 60 sts around the octagon using 5 mm double-pointed needles and black sheep heather yarn and knit 12 garters in circular garter st. Cast off.

Finishing: Darn in loose ends.

Beret: Cast on 14 sts using 7 mm needles and black sheep heather/white yarn. Knit pattern A/B in garter st. N.B.: □ = 2 sts and 2 garters. Sts are cast on or cast off in each garter in order to create an octagon as shown on chart. Cast off. Pick up 104 sts around the octagon using 5 mm circular needle and black sheep heather/white yarn and knit in circular garter st. After 5 garters, k2 together 52 times, then knit ribbing (k1, p1) 3 cm. Cast off with black sheep heather/black yarn

Finishing: Darn in loose ends.

Bag: Cast on 21 sts using 6 mm needles and black sheep heather yarn. Knit pattern A in garter st. N.B.: □ = 3 sts and 3 garters. Sts are cast on or cast off in each garter in order to create an octagon as shown on chart. When complete, cast off 3 sts on each side and continue knitting the 15 sts in the middle for the closing flap. Knit 3 garters and cast off on each side 1 st, then 2 sts in the next garter. Cast off. Knit the handle as follows: cast on 5 sts using 5 mm needles and black sheep heather yarn and knit in garter st an approx. 22 cm long strip.

Finishing: Sew side seams. Sew the edges of the handle together around the plastic tubing. Fasten both ends inside the bag. Crochet an edging around the closing flap using sc, 5 mm crochet hook and natural black yarn. Line the bag. Sew velcro strips onto bag and flap. Darn in loose ends.

23 Child's cap and mittens

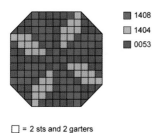

■ 1408
☐ 1404
■ 0053

☐ = 2 sts and 2 garters

Inserts: Suður-Þingeyinga District Museum, Grenjaðarstaðir.

Size: 2 (4) 6 years
Materials: Létt-lopi from Ístex
- **glacier blue heather 1404, 1 ball**
- **light red heather 1408, 1 ball**
- **camel 1400, 1 ball**
- **acorn heather 0053, 1 ball**
Needles: 4½ mm needles, 3½ mm double-pointed needles and 3 mm crochet hook
Tension: 10 x 10 cm in stocking stitch on 3½ mm needles equal 12 sts and 14 garters.
☐ = 2 sts and 2 garters
Knitting method: The mittens are knitted in the round in stocking stitch, then the thumb.
The cap is knitted back and forth using garter stitch and intarsia technique, then in the round in stocking st.
Garter stitch: 1 garter = 2 rows k worked back and forth

Cap: Cast on 14 sts using 4½ mm needles and acorn heather yarn. Knit pattern back and forth in garter st. N.B.: ☐ = 2 sts and 2 garters. Sts are cast on or cast off in each garter in order to create an octagon as shown on chart. When complete, cast off. Pick up 80 (90) 100 sts around the octagon using 3½ mm double-pointed needles and acorn heather yarn; knit in the round in stocking st 1 row with glacier blue heather yarn, then alternating acorn

heather and camel yarn 6 (8) 10 cm. Finish with camel yarn. Place the first 10 (11) 12 sts on a stitch holder or length of yarn, knit 14 (15) 16 sts for the first ear flap, place the next 32 (38) 44 sts on a stitch holder or length of yarn, knit 14 (15) 16 sts for the second ear flap and place the last 10 (11) 12 sts on a stitch holder or length of yarn. Knit the ear flap alternating acorn heather yarn and camel yarn: shape it by placing on a stitch holder or length of yarn on both sides 1 st in each row, 3 times, then in the next row 2 sts. Finish with camel yarn. Knit the other ear flap the same way. Place all the sts on the needles, knit in the round 1 row k and 1 row p with acorn heather yarn and cast off.
Finishing: Darn in loose ends.

Right mitten: Cast on 24 (26) 28 sts using 3½ mm double-pointed needles and acorn heather yarn, join in a circle on 4 needles and knit 13 (14) 15 rows ribbing (k1, p1). Continue knitting in stocking st. Increase 2 (4) 4 sts evenly spaced in the first row. Even out the sts so that half are divided between the first 2 needles and the second half on the last 2 needles. Knit 1 row with glacier blue heather yarn then alternating acorn heather yarn and camel yarn. After 7 (9) 11 rows, mark the thumb as follows: k1, knit the next 5 (5) 6 sts with a contrasting color yarn, return them to left needle and continue knitting with main color yarn. After 13 (15) 17 rows, begin decrease on mitten as follows: k2 together in each row the first 2 sts on first and third needle and the last 2 sts on second and fourth needle until there are 6 (6) 4 sts left. Break yarn and draw through the sts.
Thumb: Pull out contrasting color yarn and place the sts on 3 needles. Pick up an extra st on each side in order to prevent gaps. Divide the sts so that half are on one needle and the other half is divided between the other two needles. In the first row k2 together on each side (extra sts). After knitting 8 (10) 12 rows begin decrease as follows: k2 together in every row the first and last 2 sts on the first needle, the first 2 sts on the second needle and the last 2 sts on the third needle until there are 6 (6) 4 sts left. Break yarn and draw through the sts.
Finishing: Darn in loose ends.
Left mitten: The left mitten is knitted like the right mitten except that the thumb is knitted on the left side.

24 Narrow scarf with roses

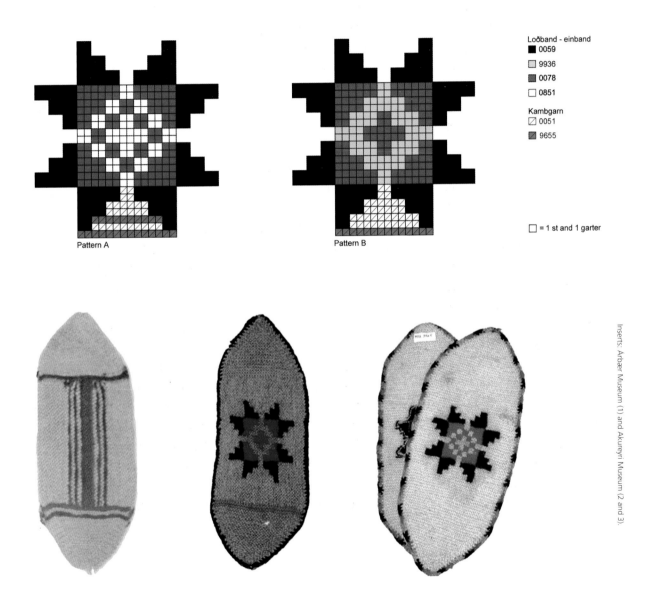

Loðband – einband
■ 0059
▨ 9936
▨ 0078
☐ 0851

Kambgarn
◩ 0051
◩ 9655

☐ = 1 st and 1 garter

Pattern A

Pattern B

Inserts: Árbær Museum (1) and Akureyri Museum (2 and 3).

155

Length: approx. 90 cm
Materials: Kambgarn from Ístex
- white 0051, 1 ball
- light blue 9655, 1 ball
- red 9664, 1 ball
Loðband - einband from Ístex
- white 0851, 1 ball
- black 0059, 1 ball
- bright red 0078, 1 ball
- light green 9936, 1 ball
Needles: 3 mm needles
Tension: 10 x 10 cm in garter stitch with Kambgarn yarn on 3 mm needles equal 23 sts and 26 garters.
□ = 1 st and 1 garter
Knitting method: The middle section is knitted lengthwise in garter stitch, then the roses using garter stitch and intarsia technique, crosswise at each end. Loðband - einband yarn is used doubled.
Garter stitch: 1 garter = 2 rows k worked back and forth

Middle section: Cast on 180 sts using 3 mm needles and white Kambgarn yarn. Knit 6 garters alternating white and blue Kambgarn yarn, 2 garters red Kambgarn yarn and 6 garters alternating blue and white Kambgarn yarn. Cast off.
Roses: Pick up 14 sts from one end of the middle section using 3 mm needles and blue yarn and knit pattern A with Kambgarn yarn and Loðband - einband yarn, doubled, as shown on chart. N. B.: □ = 1 st and 1 garter. Sts are cast on and cast off as needed to form the rose petals as shown on chart. Knit pattern B in the same way at the other end of the middle section.
Finishing: Darn in loose ends.

25 Narrow scarf with flowerpots

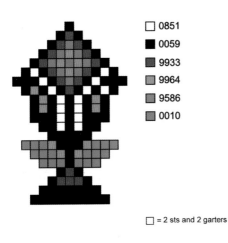

□	0851
■	0059
▦	9933
▦	9964
▦	9586
▦	0010

□ = 2 sts and 2 garters

Inserts: Elsa E. Guðjónsson (1) and Skógar District Museum (2).

Length: approx. 152 cm
Materials: Kambgarn from Ístex
- white 0051, 1 ball
- light gray 0998, 1 ball
- black 0059, 1 ball
Loðband - einband from Ístex
- white 0851, 1 ball
- black 0059, 1 ball
- violet 9933, 1 ball
- orange 9934, 1 ball
- bright green 9823, 1 ball
- blue 0010, 1 ball
Needles: 3 mm needles.

Tension: 10 x 10 cm in garter stitch with Kambgarn yarn on 3 mm needles equal 23 sts and 26 garters.

□ = 2 sts and 2 garters

Knitting method: The middle section is knitted lengthwise in garter stitch, then the flowerpots using garter stitch and intarsia technique, crosswise at each end. Loðband - einband yarn is used doubled.

Garter stitch: 1 garter = 2 rows k worked back and forth

Middle section: Cast on 320 sts using 3 mm needles and black Kambgarn yarn. Knit 6 garters black Kambgarn yarn, 2 garters white Kambgarn yarn, 2 garters gray Kambgarn yarn, 2 garters white Kambgarn yarn and 6 garters black Kambgarn yarn. Cast off.

Flowerpots: Pick up 14 sts from each end of the middle section using 3 mm needles and black Loðband - einband yarn, doubled, and knit pattern. N. B.: □ = 2 sts and 2 garters. Sts are cast on and cast off as needed to form the flowerpots as shown on chart.

Finishing: Darn in loose ends.

26 Band-weave edged potholders

□ 0051
■ 0059
▨ 0086

□ = 2 sts and 2 rows

Size: approx. 21.5 x 21.5 cm
Materials: Álafoss lopi from Ístex
- light beige 0086, 1 ball
- black 0059, 1 ball
- white 0051, 1 ball
Létt-lopi from Ístex
- black 0059, 1 ball
- white 0051, 1 ball
Needles: 4½ mm needles
Black wool fabric or linen: two patches approx. 21.5 x 21.5 cm
Tension: 10 x 10 cm using Fair Isle technique and stocking stitch on 4½ mm needles equal 18 sts and 21 rows.
☐ = 2 sts and 2 rows
Knitting technique: The potholders are knitted tightly back and forth using Fair Isle technique and stocking stitch, lined and edged using the *slynging* technique (band-weaving and sewing simultaneously) described on pages 94 and 95.

Cast on 34 sts using 4½ mm needles and light beige lopi yarn. Knit pattern in stocking st. N.B.: ☐ = 2 sts and 2 rows. Cast off. Knit a second potholder in the same way. Cut the lining the same size as the potholder. Sew potholder and lining together at the edges and topstitch lengthwise. Make a warp from 8 threads drawn together approx. 300 cm long, alternating black and white Létt-lopi yarn. Thread the weft and anchore the threads in the foot shed with a strong yarn e.g. Kambgarn yarn from Ístex. Weave an approx. 12 cm long band, then begin the *slynging*, i.e. weaving and sewing simultaneously, at a corner of the potholder and all around it. Break off yarn. Fold the 12 cm band over to create a loop and fasten it to the corner. Darn in loose ends.

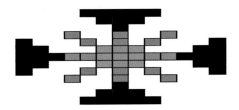